Corporate Mission Possible

The Manager's Guide to a Successful Corporate Career

Rob Mars

Copyright © 2012 Rob Mars

All rights reserved under International Copyright Conventions. This book may not be reproduced, in whole or in part, in any form or by any means electronic or mechanical, including photocopying, recording, or by any information storage and retrieval system now known or hereafter invented, without written permission from the publisher, Meet & Greet s.r.o.

3rd Edition (CreateSpace paperback) 05 /13

Published by Meet & Greet s.r.o.
info@meetandgreet.cz
Cover design & illustrations: Meet & Greet

Printed in the USA

ISBN 10: 8087694023
ISBN 13: 978-8087694022 (Meet & Greet)

Acknowledgement

Thank you to my beautiful wife for all the encouragement, support, and the illustrations throughout the book.

Thank you to Autumn J. Conley for the excellent editing.

Special thanks go to all the corporations for letting me work for them.

TABLE OF CONTENT

Introduction 5
Chapter I – Meet Mr. Corporation 11
Chapter II - The Way We Do Things Around Here 29
Chapter III – Jurassic Park 41
Chapter IV – Lingo Trap 51
Chapter V – Stretched Sails 55
Chapter VI – The Most Powerful Thing 65
Chapter VII – Counting the Beans.. 73
Chapter VIII – Answer the Question 83
Chapter IX – Rights & Wrongs 93
Chapter X – Climbing the Ladder 99
Chapter XI – Just One Life 105
Chapter XII – Mowing Your Own Lawn.................................. 113
Chapter XIII – Threshold 119
Final Words 125

Introduction

You have just told your boss she is wrong...

Instead of you, John (that incompetent asshole) has been selected to go for the seven days of sales training in Cancun...

You had a heated row with Dave, the self-proclaimed marketing guru, regarding the next budget...

You forgot to forecast an important invoice that should have come last month but has not and appeared only this month – a disaster to your results now...

You are frustrated because the financial department is bombarding you daily with requests for new statistics, spreadsheets, explanations on costs/results/outlook, and God knows what else...

You have not been able to push your expansion proposal through on the management meeting, and there is a real danger that your team will be reduced...

You did not see your children (not to mention your partner) this week, as they've already been asleep every evening when you came home and were not yet awaken when you left in the morning...

In spite of your excellent results last year, your bonus does not meet your expectations...

Your budget for next year looks like Mount Everest, and your corporate protective equipment includes neither oxygen mask nor hiking gear...

Does this jog your memory? Have you had similar experience lately?

If you have not, consider yourself a very lucky person indeed. To avoid these circumstances, you might want to forgo working in a corporation, especially with international flavor. However, if you're already employed by one of these, I am sure you are painfully familiar with a few of the above.

I have been working in the world of international corporations for most of my professional career, spanning some twenty-seven years. My personal experience, combined with the stories from peers and friends, often discussed through the past years after a couple of beers (without which we would have been too shy to discuss this topic) inspired me to write this book.

We live in a world where large, multinational corporations rule. They offer a great opportunity for a great many managers and professionals to learn, climb the ladder, and gain a healthy dose of self-fulfillment and enough financial security. They are very efficient vehicles that will enable you to drive toward your personal objectives.

As you know, however, there is no such thing as a free lunch. Corporations set their own rules and maintain their culture with accepted habits and expected behavior. They also have their own ways about things – and these are by no means trivial. To survive or – God bless! – to be successful, you will have to adhere to these. Moreover, some of them are beyond tricky, nearly unbelievable, I can tell you!

This book does not aspire to be a reference or textbook by cataloging, describing, discussing, and solving all potential obstacles the aspiring corporate manager-to-be or manager can possibly meet during his or her career. Instead, it serves as a guide to explore the most important obstacles and find solutions for handling them successfully; every tidbit of advice you might find within these pages comes from personal experience and words of wisdom I've gleaned from others along the way.

The following chapters will guide you through the most important areas that you must master if you are to become a seasoned corporate "veteran." Likewise, they will equip you to spend a long career in this environment:

- **Chapter I: Meet Mr. Corporation** – Whether you find yourself in a large corporation by your own decision or by chance, you should be prepared to comply with basic rules; you will not even survive without knowing and adhering to these.

- **Chapter II: The Way We Do Things Around Here** – Studying the culture and understanding cultural differences will make you feel at home. Think of it like moving to a different country where you would like to live.
- **Chapter III: Jurassic Park** – How can you find your way in the jungle of matrix organizations?
- **Chapter IV: Lingo Trap** – It is high time to learn the local dialect!
- **Chapter V: Stretched Sails** – Do you know where your corporation is heading and why? It is quite useful so that you do not drive the opposite direction.
- **Chapter VI: The Most Powerful Thing** – What is the most valuable asset to get your hands on in the corporation?
- **Chapter VII: Counting the Beans** – Money, money, money…
- **Chapter VIII: Answer the Question** – Local dialect is not enough. Learn to communicate properly
- **Chapter IX: Rights and Wrongs** – The bright and shady sides of corporate ethics
- **Chapter X: Climbing the Ladder** – How high can you safely go?
- **Chapter XI: Just One Life** – Do not miss your life making your career
- **Chapter XII: Mowing Your Own Lawn** – Read this before you decide to quit working for someone else and start your own company.

- **Chapter XIII: Threshold** – Keep your principles and self-respect intact – always.

Working for a corporation is not the ideal job for everyone. While many people are attracted to the corporate world, there is a high probability that it is not always a good fit, a good match. Hence, the less "corporate capable" will ultimately leave on their own initiative or will be kindly (or not so kindly) advised to do so. A lot of stress, energy, and tears could be saved if employees were aware of what obstacles their choice might entail.

Even if you are an adaptable person, it will take you years to learn "the corporate way." Should you, for some reason, change companies during those years, you will have to start again – maybe not from the beginning, but at least halfway. Each corporation has its own unwritten "white book," and it might cost you sweat and tears to learn them. Unfortunately, most corporations do not hand you a copy of their playbook when you get onboard.

If I could have read this book some twenty-five years ago, I would not have made so many mistakes along the way. Thus, I implore you to spare yourself embarrassment in your future career as a corporate citizen/manager and learn from the mistakes of others. If this book helps even one of you find less frustration, more fun, and easier climbing of the corporate ladder, I have fulfilled my mission here.

Corporate Mission Possible

Chapter I – Meet Mr. Corporation

Suppose you've just joined the corporation you want to work at for the rest of your life. Perhaps this was something you sought relentlessly, or maybe it was not by your choice at all. How did it happen? Was it up to you – or someone else?

Corporate Mission Possible

There are two basic ways to become part of a corporation. Either you decide to seek employment there and land the job, or you just so happen to work for a company that is acquired by a corporation. The difference is significant.

If *you* decide to join a corporation, it is your choice. Perhaps you have read or heard good things about the company, and they just so happened to have a job opening that interested you. You might think joining a large organization is a great opportunity, which it most certainly can be. You assume you'll learn a lot and that you'll be able to make a career out of it, earning a decent living in the process. Perhaps you've found yourself in the unique situation, wherein the experience you are offering is too specific to be used in a smaller organization. To utilize your rare, keen, specialized abilities to the maximum potential, you are predestined to work for a large organization (e.g. experienced senior managers, ambitious young people who want to be managers, specialized engineers with high qualifications, HR/finance professionals, multilingual folks, and so on).

Whatever your reason, if you choose to work for a corporation, you only have one last chance to make sure it's a good fit – that you and the corporation will mutually benefit from you joining them. To accomplish this, try to learn as much as possible about the culture of the corporation during the interview process. Ask questions about your future responsibilities and your supposed authority over people and projects. I am sure there will be a lot of the first, while the latter can be more difficult.

Some years ago, Danny K., a good friend of mine, decided to search for a new challenge. He had been working as a senior executive for a corporation, and he began to realize that the authority to which he was subjected was quite strict. He often felt like a puppet, even a prisoner at times. Important matters were decided at least one level up, strategy was presented to him instead of being discussed with him, and the only thing expected from him was execution. Danny was given no allowance to make strategic decisions or answer questions without the permission of his superiors, and that was a long and painstaking process in and of itself. His authority was, in fact, limited to operational management. Considering that he had twenty years of successful company management under his belt, this was not acceptable. Unfortunately, Danny did not expect this; he didn't see it before joining up with the corporation he now found himself in, and he didn't think to ask, assuming he'd be granted all the authority and decision-making power he needed when the time came.

During the search for a different job, Danny was interviewed by a large corporation looking for a senior executive. The corporation had a respected brand name and a widely known presence in almost every country in the world. It seemed as if it would be an honor to work for such a company. Having learned his lesson, Danny found out that a friend had left the company not long ago and asked him about the culture there. My friend did not believe his ears when he realized that this company was much the same. Managers had limited authority and struggled with frustration when trying to get decisions from superiors on non-standard issues. They had to report in two lines of direction in the matrix organization; these quite often crossed each other. No creativity was expected from them in strategic matters either. After he confirmed this with careful questions during the interview process, he decided to look elsewhere.

As mentioned, you might also end up working for a corporation if you work for a smaller company that is ultimately gobbled up by a larger one, a corporation. In this case, it is not your choice. It just...happens – and, mind you, it happens quite often. Globalization, mergers, and acquisitions drive business concentration. We experience this phenomenon in abundance in the developing countries: Global companies enter the scene and get to the local market by acquisition. When the corporation buys a smaller local company, not only is immediate market presence acquired (this is a favorable way to buy starting market shares), but also local market knowledge, special technology, products, and personnel.

People working for a small company that is "annexed" this way by a large multinational face a major change:

>INSTEAD OF WORKING FOR JOHN, THE PREVOIUS OWNER,
>
>YOU WILL BE WORKING FOR MR. CORPORATION

The change will represent major challenges. You will have to adopt a different culture, change your habits and maybe even your language. You will need to learn new procedures and rules and must get used to providing detailed written reports by specific and strictly held deadlines. On the other hand, the new owner will find opportunities that you'd never dreamt of: new markets, new products, new technologies, etc. Is it a good deal? Is it worth the trade-off and all those pesky changes and do-overs? Most of us would say it certainly is. However, based on my experience, in reality, the answer is more complicated.

If your company is annexed, you do not have too much of a choice. Your employment changes without your assent, and mostly not in a formal fashion. Your contract will likely remain the same, as will your salary. However, you may start to feel after a time that you have joined a new company. Your depth of experience will determine where you reside in the company hierarchy. If you are a director, the truth is, you may be kindly asked to leave. If you are middle management or one of the professionals (engineers), you will bear firsthand witness to all the changes happening around you: the rules, the behavior, the reports, the company software, the products, the requirements, the objectives – everything. Your boss may not even be an exception.

Chapter I - Meet Mr. Corporation

You will need to evaluate, learn the new things, and decide whether this new cup of tea is yours. If it is not, you can decide to leave and try elsewhere. Of course this is easier said than done. You may not be in a position to choose if you have a family to support, a mortgage to pay, or you're simply not the type who does well switching jobs or finding new ones easily. You may have never tried to find another job before. Anyway, that great, newly merged company can be full of opportunities. So what will you need to do to stay and work well within the new parameters? Plenty!

You'll have to learn not only the new rules, the new software, and the new products, but also how to adjust yourself to the new requirements. How do you need to behave to be viewed as a worthy member of the team? You used to see John, the previous owner, every day, and you knew that a change in the curve of his brow was a warning, a sign of danger and dissatisfaction. You knew exactly how to behave to please your boss, and he told you directly when he was not happy with your performance and gave you suggestions as to how to improve. But how do you make Mr. Corporation happy so you can keep your job? How can you make a faceless somebody or something happy if it has no expression, no furrowing brow? Who cannot smile and cannot shout? An entity about whom you do not know anything? Is it possible to learn this? Is it possible to learn how to behave and act in the corporate world?

THIS BOOK IS HERE TO HELP YOU –

NOT ONLY SURVIVE BUT ALSO TO SUCCEED!

We will not discuss being incapable and needing to find ways to hole up and stay under the radar to survive. Even being a top performer cannot 100 percent guarantee that you will have a long-term career in the corporation. Why is that? Is it not performance that really counts?

Corporate Mission Possible

Yes, performance is one of the main factors to ensure success in the corporate world. Nevertheless, are you sure your performance can be *seen* to those who will ultimately decide your fate? Are you sure they will notice your efforts? What other aspects are taken into account at your daily work and, in the end, during your annual appraisal?

Personnel evaluation is an art in the corporation. There are whole departments tasked with seeking the best methods by which to judge you and recommend to your superiors, ways of measuring and evaluating you. Often, potential is given much higher consideration than current performance. This is quite similar to the stock market: a new company, yet to show good results but exhibiting major potential, is often more attractive to investors than a reliable, performing, mature company. If you are at the top of your career, your future development can be limited. You are able to perform now, but for how long? How can you demonstrate that there are still opportunities for you? How will you show them that there still exist attributes and personality traits that are worth investing in and that will bring rich rewards in a couple of years?

A family friend, Greg B., was fifty years old when he faced the biggest challenge in his employment history at a corporate job in his middle managerial position. He had always been a good, knowledgeable performer; however, that knowledge and experience had reached its zenith. To his employer, it seemed improbable that Greg would be able to develop significantly further. A newly hired young employee, although at the start of his career, with contemporary knowledge but lack of experience, had been showing below standard performance. However, the young person showed huge enthusiasm and offered very open-minded, creative thinking, though his notions seemed utterly crazy at first. He has also improved his performance from 70 to 90 percent in the past half-year, and he was willing to work twelve hours every day if necessary. The employer promoted the young employee in time, and when it came to decide who is more valuable for the corporation, the decision fell in support of the younger employee over Greg. After fifteen years of loyal service to the company, the more experienced Greg was laid off.

Do not be mistaken: It is not about age, though the above example was only shared to indicate the possible extremes. Of course, being young and energetic doesn't make you a shoo-in either; if you are young but do not show the required characteristics, you will not be valued optimally. If this is the case, you will eventually fall behind in the career flow. Perhaps you're perfectly okay with your current position and claim you really have no interest in ridiculous ladder-climbing, but this is a huge mistake! Some corporations have a system where the highest 10 percent at appraisals get an above-average pay raise, the 80 percent in the middle get an average raise, and the lowest 10 percent get only a pink slip and are shown the door. Remember this:

> THERE IS A LADDER WHETHER YOU LIKE IT OR NOT.
>
> IF YOU'RE NOT CLIMBING UP IT, YOU ARE GOING DOWN!

Even worse, you can be tossed off the ladder very easily by those above you and shoved out of the way by those trying to climb over you.

Opening

Employees with relevant experience tend to be inaccessible to new ideas, for these seem to somehow threaten their respected knowledge and position – particularly when those ideas come from younger colleagues or employees with less experience in the specific field. These employees rely on their vast experience and view all new ideas with suspicion: "Well, it has never been tried before... It's too risky... Nobody does it like that in this branch of the industry... We'll have to change too many things to implement that..." and so on. In an entrepreneurial environment of a large corporation,

THIS MENTALITY CAN BE FATAL!

You should always be open to new ideas. Instead of criticizing them or instantly ranting about how unreasonable they are, you should discuss the practical ways in which they might prove beneficial. Be open to their potential. If you are a knowledgeable expert in the field, your opinion will be taken seriously, but only if you offer it in a positive way, with an attitude that shows you have the company's best interests in mind, even if that requires change. You can use new ideas as an opportunity to show how your experience can be invaluable to optimize its benefits, because you know how the new plans can realistically fit and be put to good use. In this way, instead of booting yourself out, you will strengthen your position.

I will caution you, however, to be careful with new ideas coming from the corporation itself. These can be dangerous to you if you are not open to changes and adaptations. You must embrace these ideas and serve as their advocate. You have to be creative and genuine in your support of corporation endeavors, as you do not want anyone to think there is some sinister or selfish hidden agenda in your support.

John W. was a very intelligent engineering manager of a small local company. He had been working for the company for ten years when it was bought out by a large multinational corporation. He had difficulty accepting and consuming the new culture, all the new requirements, new methodologies, and new ways of thinking. Nevertheless, John managed remarkably well in the end, despite the fact that he was already fifty at the time of the acquisition and that he had never worked for a corporation before. In the beginning, his opposing manner was cautious and subtle. He was reserved in discussions and maintained his opinion but opened a gate for the potential of new ideas. Later he realized the necessity of a more assertive behavior and more open support for development. He started to act as an advocate for new technology, new methods of quality assurance, and updated manufacturing procedures that came from the corporation. At the same time, he came with own ideas based on his vast engineering experience in the specific field. As a result, he became a very respected and successful engineering manager of the corporation. Not only did John survive, but he also took a positive next step in his career, garnering him the title of director in a research and development company – an even larger corporation that took over part of the previous corporation's local operations a couple years later.

Asking

Attentive listening during discussions is good, but asking intelligent questions is even better. Never underestimate how important it is to show your interest: If you ask, it shows that you *want* to learn. If you ask intelligent, well-thought-out questions, you will also show that you are thinking deeply about the matters under discussion. Smart questions indicate that although you are very knowledgeable (you are able to assess the topic, get to the important aspect, and address the significant issues), you are also ready, willing, and able to extend your knowledge. You also show that

> YOU WANT TO BE PART OF THE THING.

One successful managerial technique involves nothing other than asking the right questions. Challenging ideas (without destroying them), exploring the depth of a method or thought, motivating others to think about aspects of the matter not discussed before – all these are proactive methods in a discussion to find optimal solutions for the problem. You do not need to go to the end yet in the beginning. You might be a junior member of the team. If you are, it's likely that nobody expects you to form the conclusion after getting the right answers and analyzing and synthesizing them. At this stage, it is enough that you ask the right, smart questions, thus indicating your intelligence, your attachment to the dilemma, and your interest. Rest assured if you do this, the time will come when you can demonstrate your further abilities.

Showing

Most corporations highly value enthusiasm. It shows interest, attachment, and ardor, and involvement on the part of the employee. It means he or she is committed, interested, and motivated to go the extra mile in reaching objectives, even beyond expectation. The employee may not yet show documented results, but potential and motivation, indicated by enthusiasm, predestines that employee for a great future in the corporation.

If you happen to be an unenthusiastic sort of person, do not show it. In general, negative behavior and attitude is not welcome in any corporation. You are expected to understand the corporate strategy and its objectives and work toward them, even when that strategy is not properly or clearly communicated. Those who fail to do so may not have a long life in that corporation. We will discuss later what you should do if the strategy is difficult to surmise or is not evident.

Be sure, however, that you don't exhibit false enthusiasm. This can be dangerous. Your superiors are not stupid. If you act as if you have a burning spirit for the corporation and your actions lack the drive to back it up, this will be counterproductive. If you never stay after five p.m., even when many of your colleagues stay to handle month's end, closings, or shipping of urgent customer orders, your enthusiasm will be seen as an act, and it will eventually work against you. The same is true with overdone enthusiasm. If you are overexcited by each and every new idea from your boss, if you exclaim in meetings, "Oh, I love it! Just think of all the great things we can do with this!" you will fall under suspicion or will simply become a laughingstock not only to your colleagues, but also to your superiors.

The measure of the right enthusiasm is different in different cultures. In American and Latin corporations, a higher level of expressed enthusiasm is expected and required than in, say, a German company. You may have heard the adage that the extent of a smile, from mouth corner to mouth corner, varies in inches, America's four to Germany's two. The same can be said for enthusiasm.

Over-exaggerated enthusiasm can cause employees to ignore or disrespect important rules and guidelines. It can trigger unwanted creativity as well – or at least this is how it is looked upon in the corporation. You will have to find the right measure by which your enthusiasm is perceived positively and helps you position yourself for success instead of creating enemies.

Acting

Perform! "What advice," you say. "As if I didn't already know that." This should be trivial for a workplace, especially if you have ambitions to make a corporate career. But let's just look at an example.

My schoolmate, Brad R., is a talented engineer who also has some managerial ambitions and skills. He worked hard for several years in a corporation, bested his colleagues in the number of patents, managed successful projects, and helped to introduce new products. Eventually, Brad was promoted to engineering manager. At that point, Brad determined it was time to enjoy the fruits of his hard work, and he began taking things a bit less seriously. He spent fewer hours at work, preferring to hit the golf course instead. As a result, his success at work became very average, never again excelling beyond the budgeted level. After a year, Brad was fired.

> "YOU ARE ONLY AS GOOD AS YOUR LAST QUARTER RESULTS."

You may hear this in your corporation, as I used to hear it some years ago. Steady performance, with systematic, constant improvement, is expected in most companies, corporations included. While enthusiasm, open-mindedness, creativity, and intelligence are important, none of these are a substitute for consistent good performance – at least not for long. Performance is the base of your corporate life: a necessary (albeit insufficient in most cases) condition for your success. You must always be acting, always be performing, if you intend to stay long enough to get ahead.

Presenting

I met tens of hardworking, well-performing employees, professionals, and middle management during my corporate career, none of whom had ever climbed more than one or two steps of the ladder. Some haven't even moved at all. One reason was because they were unable to present their results (i.e. themselves) properly – or at all, for that matter.

I cannot emphasize enough the importance of presentation. Some people are shy and hope it will be enough to perform – that their results will speak for themselves. Unfortunately, this is seldom the case. Results can go unnoticed, either because there are enough good results around to compete with yours, or simply because their importance is not revealed to those who matter. Thus, you must grab all reasonable opportunities to show evidence of how good you are.

> SHYNESS HAS NO VALUE IN THE CORPORATION.

Of course, this does not mean you should be a braggart, always boasting your results to anybody who cares to listen. Inform your boss about all milestones of your work. If you make a presentation of your project's progress, show your achievements as facts. Do not forget to give tribute to all colleagues who helped you reach those discoveries, and they will return the favor and acknowledge you when they make their own presentations.

Imagine that you spent a year working on a project, delving into it, and spending a great deal of time and thought working toward a particular result. Would you expect a bonus or at least some accolades? How would you feel if you received none, simply because your results were not presented well and went unnoticed? I am relatively certain you'd feel slighted. I know I would.

Even if you inform your boss about the partial achievements of your work during the year, make a record of each achievement for yourself. This log will play an important role in your annual appraisal. Remind your supervisor of these during the appraisal; they may very well help to balance out your less successful ventures. If you do not remind your boss of your achievements, he or she may very well only remember the failures.

STOP JUSTIFYING YOURSELF!

On the other hand, if your results cannot speak for themselves, they are not good enough. Criticism in the corporation is a positive thing, and you should not take it lightly. The frequent practice of standing up and justifying your results, explaining the obstacles, and correcting critical interpretation is counterproductive. Criticism is the mirror that reality places in front of you. If you are not able to see yourself in the clear light, you are squandering the opportunity to improve. Take criticism humbly and make plans to improve and present the results of these efforts. Committing to improvement is much more valuable than defending your not-so-convincing results. Your future is even more valuable for the corporation than your present.

Understanding

The most important paradox of communication is: "It is not important what message you wanted to convey to somebody. It is important what he or she understood."

We often believe we have explained our message to the receiving party sufficiently and that they have understood our meaning. In most cases, however, we do not even bother to make sure of this. Numerous books have been written about communication, and it is not within the scope of this book to substitute for those. Nevertheless, as communication plays an important role in the life and processes of corporations, it also has a deciding power in your ability to succeed.

Not long ago, I hired a project manager to do a job in an environment where he had to communicate daily with customers, colleagues from other departments, and vendors and suppliers. He was very successful with customers; they loved him. He was hard on suppliers, but he managed to get deliveries on time and succeeded in acquiring some valuable discounts. However, he completely failed with colleagues. He looked down his nose at them, was arrogant, and always made sure to brag about his many years of experience. At the same time, he was unable to master the technical details of the products, even after several months; he had to rely on the experience of the colleagues from the technical department in order for him to complete building offers, a vital part of his job. Thanks much to his uppity attitude toward his co-workers, they were, of course, less than helpful. After six months, he resigned, just before I got to the point of firing him.

Maintaining a proper balance of communication is vital, whether it is to your boss, your customers, your colleagues, or your subordinates. It is absolutely mandatory for success.

There are some basic rules you will have to keep. You will have to decide on the communication method based on who the addressee is and what level of information you want to transmit. Sometimes a phone call is more effective and desirable than e-mail. You certainly do not want to convey sensitive or highly confidential information electronically, as that would require a face-to-face meeting. While you may be very articulate, you will want to adjust your tone and your words based on who it is that you are speaking with; in other words, the people on the shop floor of the factory might be addressed differently than the CEO of the company or a customer. Mastering at least the basic rules of effective communication will be a key for your success in the corporation.

Maturing

This piece of advice concerns, more or less, the generation below forty years of age, though there are examples of immature behavior in even much older individuals.

Maturity in corporations involves the following:

ALWAYS THINK BEFORE TALKING

Also remember that you shouldn't necessarily blurt out everything that you have on your mind. Your words can be used to judge you. You might recall the Miranda rights, "Anything you say *can* and *will* be used against you..." (And hopefully you only recall it from a television show or something you learned in school!) This warning applies to the corporate world as much as it does to possible criminals, and careful communication is a sign of maturity..

Control your emotions! The corporate environment can sometimes be extremely frustrating. You are entitled to personal ideals and philosophies, but these may or may not be respected within the corporation. The rules might seem restricting and even stupid or unnecessary. The behavior and attitudes of some of your colleagues or superiors may seem arrogant and inconsiderate. Your internal moral compass might advise you to react harshly and refuse ideas, actions, and opinions. Think first. Answer from a detached view, don't offend the other party, and grant others the opportunity to be right once in a while.

Letting your frustration control your words and actions is the worst thing you can do in these circumstances. Especially younger employees, who do not have sufficient experience in controlling their emotions, can destroy themselves and their promising corporate career via unsolicited and inappropriate comments or answers. Controlling your emotions is an art that comes partially from age and experience, but it can also be developed. If you believe you are emotional or quick-tempered, finding couching courses of self-control may be an excellent idea.

Several years ago, I was asked to manage a major improvement project in a manufacturing division. The level of quality was far from satisfactory, the culture did not support improvement actions, and processes were euphemistically suboptimal. I succeeded in implementing several changes that significantly improved output quality and decreased poor quality claims three-fold. I was on a good path to reach steady improvements after only five months. Still, there was a high risk of quality failures that could seriously affect sales and customer perception. One of these failures actually occurred, and in light of it, I was visited by the CEO. In that meeting, he demanded that I commit to a one-and-a-half order of quality improvement in the next five months. He wanted to decrease the DPM (defect per million) from over 100,000 to less than 10,000. My reaction? I almost quit. I wanted to tell him that what he wanted was impossible and would require years of hard work. After a heated discussion, during which I was almost fired, my colleagues convinced me to show my ultimate commitment and "sign a blank check," stating that the improvement would happen as requested. I stayed, and in the end, we improved quality to 5,000 DPM in only a year's time.

I understood only after several years that the intention of the CEO was not to make me commit literally to the numbers he'd mentioned; what he wanted was an unlimited personal commitment to results beyond expectation. He became frustrated when I seemed unwilling. He thought I made excuses of missing culture, need of time to set up motivation system, change of procedures, stabilizing already reached level of improvement, etc. I allowed my heated emotions to surface during that discussion (rather a nasty row), and that caused him to think I might have been too immature and incompetent for the job. Evidently, it was a major mistake to behave as I did, for I was threatened with the loss of my job. Fortunately, my more mature and experienced colleagues convinced me how to go about things. When I agreed to the impossible target, that triggered a commitment in me to reach significant results (well, that and the portion of always necessary luck). Although I did not reach the required level in two months, the progress proved that the commitment was there, a very positive trend indeed. The CEO did not ask me about progress until six to eight months later, and by that time, we had gotten really very close to his dictated targets. Not only did he accept that, but I was eventually promoted to a job with higher responsibility.

 ## Chapter Takeaways

• There is a difference between joining a corporation by your own free will or being forced into it when your company is acquired by a larger corporation. However, in both cases, you need to be prepared for a specific environment.

- If your current company is annexed by a corporation, prepare for major changes in everything
- There are many important rules to follow to pave your success in your corporate career:

  o Be open to new ideas and combine them with yours.

  o Ask smart questions to show your interest, intelligence, and ability to grow and learn.

  o Show the right level of true enthusiasm, depending on the corporate culture.

  o Perform! Remember: "You are only as good as your last quarter results."

  o Present your results, but do not justify. You have to advertise yourself, but be open to criticism and react appropriately.

  o Communicate properly, always keeping in mind the most effective way of communication depending on the context.

  o Be mature! Think twice before speaking or acting and control your emotions.

Chapter II - The Way We Do Things Around Here

Chapter II - The Way We Do Things Around Here

Large, multinational corporations, in most cases, exhibit culture, values, and norms that are quite different from the privately held or family businesses. Their size, the complexity of the organization, specific processes evolving in this environment – these create a unique world in which the layman can be lost.

To understand the culture of the corporation is mandatory in order to orient yourself and find the best ways of successful behavior as an employee. The corporate culture is often defined as "the way we do things around here" – structure, procedures, habits, values, relationships, and hierarchy or its lack. Globalization unifies most of this in large multinationals. Nevertheless, the culture of a corporation depends much on its origin or where the headquarters reside and the leadership is coming from. My experience comes from American, British, German, and French corporations (and their mixed culture). Major differences exist based on field of activity, but the national characteristics are dominant.

The real issue is not whether you prefer the French or hate the British, for the sake of example only (these could easily be interchanged for any nationality, if you like). The problem is that those "mother" cultures meet and crush the local culture of the new subsidiary. In the nineties, it happened in Eastern Europe or Malaysia; recently, the same has occurred in Indonesia, Brazil, and the Ukraine. Are you able to cope with the cultural differences? Is it negligible? Is there any advice to follow?

A cautionary warning: The next section, while cataloging these corporate cultures, does not offer an in-depth analysis and specific scientific value, so do not search for it. Consider the following passages as the insight of a person who has encountered these corporate cultures when these large multinationals have entered a new country. They overruled the local cultures in small companies that they purchased or set their own company culture anew as established green field subsidiaries. Do not let yourself be duped by the proclaimed propositions of corporate values as to how important the local culture is.

Chapter II - The Way We Do Things Around Here

American Culture

The American corporate culture I personally encountered as a manager could best be best characterized by the terms of pragmatism, close operational and financial control, and directness in communication and behavior. Companies work almost around the clock – and not in three shifts. You may be expected to work long hours, even on weekends.

I was indeed surprised when I appeared, dressed in a three-piece suit, at an interview with the responsible VP of one of these American companies. He wore a collared t-shirt and chino trousers and sat comfortably, casually crossing his left leg on the right. All went well, but at the end of the interview, he told me to leave the suit behind when I came to work. I spent about $1,000 in the following months to change and upgrade (or downgrade, rather) my professional wardrobe, especially after noticing that all of the managers in the mother company wore almost exclusively Ralph Lauren shirts. I still hear my wife commenting about my shirts with the polo player on them.

The CEO of the American corporation visited our subsidiary in the summer to meet 1,000 local employees and the management. I could not believe he showed up in cotton Bermuda shorts and a t-shirt!

Another CEO in a different company arrived for such a visit in suit and tie: he had inquired about local habits and had been advised that in that part of Europe (as in Germany) we wore suits and ties for meetings. Of course he was the only one, as we'd all already been transformed to "stile Americano."

An interesting article I found on the Web advises: "Always dress like the vice presidents – always." (http://www.filebox.vt.edu/users/hingram/corporation.htm) I suppose this is decent advice. The problem with CEOs is that they seem to be unpredictable.

Discussions in American company meetings do not last long. Presentations often have ten slides rather than seventy. Pragmatic solutions prevail and are implemented in short order. This might surprise more sophisticated employees, who think they have additional arguments that should be taken into consideration and often aren't. In fact, I heard the famous Nike athletic shoe slogan "Just do it" several times in one of the companies I worked for. Nothing else illustrates better the culture of some American corporations, at the same time revealing a very tight connection to sports.

DON'T TALK ABOUT IT. JUST DO IT.

This is a difficult idea for some of us to grasp. Managers like to think they are hired to use their intellectual capabilities to make the right decisions in directing organizations and companies toward objectives. If you hear, "Just do it," you might think you are only there to execute – that all decisions are made by others and you are simply a robot to carry out those orders. Your motivation may, therefore, dissipate day by day. But hold on! You have to understand that this is not meant as a slight against you. It is just the pragmatic nature of the American corporation: There are things not worth discussing, and they just need to be done. It's nothing personal, and it shouldn't be taken that way. You are a good manager who is capable of making good decisions, but sometimes it is more practical just to execute. Swallow your pride and...just do it! Moreover, if you get good at it, you may even be in for a nice bonus big enough to buy you several new pairs of Nikes. So just do it!

Large American corporations boast "business operating systems" involving well-worked-out procedures, reporting, and accountability – the joy of the systematic manager. It is less pleasant, though, to go on an hour-long conference call to explain the deviations of the results from the initial forecast. And, boy, do they go into details! Be prepared to answer ten times more questions than it is possible to ask during the hour; don't let them catch you with your pants down, for that would be most embarrassing. You are expected to know what you are doing, why you are doing it, and what the outcomes of those efforts are. If you do not know your numbers and the reasons why they are what they are, you are doomed.

British Culture

Like the English language shared by the Brits and Americans, the people can be very different and very similar to those on the other side of the ocean. Brits seem to be more formal in the workplace in the beginning but like to go for a beer (or two or three…) after the long hours. They are extremely hardworking – at least that was the case for those I met. Being European (although off the main continent), they have a better understanding for cultural differences – not that this understanding would extend to acceptance in the corporate culture.

The British are conservative, even in operational business. Changing procedures and rules is a tedious job, unless the company decides to take on some of the Japanese or American continuous improvement culture. Still, adapting lean manufacturing technique and change of culture in one of the British automotive brands took ten long years. However, after they conserved a new culture, it improved their quality and efficiency far beyond expectation. Before that, as the joke said, you purchased a car of that brand only once. Now they boast ever-improving sales and a rectified reputation.

When talking to the British, you have to take into account their unwillingness to put things bluntly on the table. They may tell you, "This idea probably is not the most optimal way of solving the issue at hand." In reality, what they mean to say is, "Forget it. This idea is absolute crap." If they say, "Excellent!" it's likely that they really mean to tell you, "Um…I suppose it's okay." These things change with the age and education of your British counterparts and can especially differ depending on industry. Younger generations tend to be more open and pragmatic, but they remain very polite in all forms of communication. Even a rather serious reprimand can seem like a pleasant discussion. Therefore, when dealing with British culture in a corporation or otherwise, you should be most cautious of the content between the lines. In most sophisticated discussions, the true intention may go unsaid, so be on the lookout! As was said by the famed Winston Churchill:

> "WE ARE THE MASTERS OF THE UNSAID WORDS
>
> BUT SLAVES OF THOSE WE LET SLIP OUT."

Latin (French/Spanish/Italian) Culture

There are many differences in cultures of multinationals originating in the above nations. Nevertheless, they – as their language and national culture – significantly differ from that of Anglo-Saxon and German peoples. Latin people are, in general, more friendly and easygoing. They enjoy talking and make their judgments based not only on facts, but also on feelings. Emotional behavior is characteristic in personal and business relations. Although current managers in Latin multinationals have a mixed business education and past (likely having studied and served in different countries and companies of the Anglo-Saxon, German, or even Japanese cultures), they cannot leave their origins behind.

The meetings are longer, sometimes involving heated discussions as spicy as the dishes made in the kitchens of these nations. Facts are important, but their presentation is as important as their existence. I always had a feeling that in a Latin environment, it is more important to build personal connections; these are then decisive in the results of commercial negotiations. I am not saying the whole Latin corporate world behaves according to Vito Corleone's principles, but the role of communication and personal relationships are emphasized. By the way, please take no offense if you are a Latin reader! In my opinion, it is more important to understand how our environment perceives us than our own belief, that we must consider how we look to the outside. In addition, there is nothing wrong with cultural differences, including the fact certain people place more value on personal relationships than on pure facts and statistical data. Consider, for the sake of example, an enthusiastic new employee. Because he is a beginner in the company or the industry, his results fall below expectations. His enthusiasm is well noticed, however, and his superiors believe it is a worthy asset in which to invest. The big truth is that you can learn the trade but not the fever pitch you feel for the business in question. This is also acknowledged in American culture but more applied in the Latin world.

German (Central European) Culture

It is a cliché that Germans are very detailed, driven by well-developed rules, love hierarchy, practice cold personal relationships, and are very effective in technical matters. However, it is quite true that German corporate culture is based on sophisticated structures, procedures, and hierarchy of organizations. No wonder the use of first names is not customary in the German business world. Calling one's business partner "Herr X" or "Frau Y," even after ten years of successful and close relationship, emphasizes formality, seriousness, and mainly mutual respect. Using the same formal titles for subordinates and employees indicates the same. Do not try using first names in a German corporation unless you are really in comradeship with the other party. It took me several years to call any of my colleagues by their first names, even after being in daily contact and sharing several dinners and beers.

Formal behavior is also expressed in business attire. Suits and tie for men and business suits for women are more common in German business culture, especially when attending important business meetings. The importance of formal contracts, well established on the legal side, is a must. When you work in a German corporation, your best bet is to thoroughly study the written formal procedures and adhere to them. This way, you cannot be mistaken.

Formal education and titles are also well respected among Germans. These will serve as no replacement for the lack of suitable results, but it will afford you initial respect, giving you credit in advance. It all depends on how you are able to use it. On the other hand, long-term experience can also replace formal education.

Your efforts to build trust and reliability will pay off in the German corporation. You can build successful relationships, business or otherwise, with the right, straight, trustful, and reliable attitude. To succeed, you must play by the rules, be sincere, and exhibit high moral standards in general, in either business or collegial relations.

In the German corporation, speaking the language is a great plus. In large German multinationals, English is the corporate language, but if you have a good grasp on German, it will prove to be an invaluable benefit. You will be one of them! So brush up your high school or university German when you are about to enter a German corporation, as this will help you build strong, valuable relationships and ease your way not only up the ladder, but also into the hearts of your colleagues, who are not at all as cold as people generally believe.

Chapter II - The Way We Do Things Around Here

Mixed Cultures

In our global corporate world, multinationals also globalize. While they will originate in one particular country, global capitalization, mergers and acquisitions, and change of ownership will have an effect on the ruling culture within the company walls. A company may start as a German company, and, over the decades, may be acquired by a larger French company with a European or Latin presence. This enterprise may later merge with an American corporation. Ownership ratios or other aspects may decide where the headquarters will then be, and most importantly, where the leadership will come from. So what will the culture of this company become? Will it retain the original German characteristics? Will it be completely taken over by American pragmatism and detailed operational management? How much Latin influence will be conserved?

However prevailing any one of the cultures are, tracks of the original culture remain preserved in the original countries. This is caused by the people who remain in the organization after mergers, the environment that is composed of the suppliers and customers, the legal system, and the social environs. Should you plan on joining a large multinational and you find it has a history of mixed culture, be aware that some remains of the original cultures may be still present. These will significantly modify the required behavior, habits, and values, even if they are not officially proclaimed. Hidden habits and values are especially worth investigating, as their latency but still vivid validity in everyday life can ease or obstruct your way up the ladder. Neglecting these can be very dangerous and ultimately fatal.

An American financial professional joined an originally German/French and finally American corporation somewhere in Europe. As their senior financial analyst in France, she presumed, as most would, that due to the headquarters being in the U.S., she would have no problem understanding the needs of the job. She knew well how to install the procedures necessary to improve financial reporting and ensure minimization of risk in the forecasts and budgets.

After some months of working in France, she was surprised to find that she was having difficulty with getting her message through to some of her team, although she was a well-known straight communicator. She even began to suspect that some members of her team hated her or were trying to sabotage her. She tried to sit down with them and make clear what is going on, but those discussions led nowhere. She was at a loss. Her superiors grew increasingly impatient with the lack of improvements in her area, and she promptly received a first warning...

You do not need to be very creative to imagine where this may have led for the naïve American professional trying to work in France. If you want to succeed in the above environment, you should not forget the role of people. She evidently did not find the right communication with her subordinates and peers. She did not build up allies because she did not understand their expectations in relationships. She simply did not put enough effort into finding the best way to succeed in the labyrinth of people relationships, communication, and culture.

Of course, you can choose the hard way. You can decide to start trying to change the people around you instead of changing yourself. Your superiors will accept this as an adequate action in a situation with unacceptable results. It will take you several new people and several months, perhaps even a year or more, to build up a synergistic team that will be able to work according to your style and achieve the required results. All the others will give in and will keep their mouth shut, fading into passive resistance. You will need extreme efforts to keep the efficiency and the results every month,

Chapter II - The Way We Do Things Around Here

every quarter. You will have to be absolutely error-free. Unless you are an extremely strong person, this will destroy you in a couple of years.

So what's the easier solution? Simple:

FIND THE RIGHT LOCAL CULTURAL ASPECTS.

These can help you reach of your subordinates and peers. Be cautious in your communication. Study their reactions and try to understand them within the parameters of French and German cultural aspects. You may need to stay with the formal Mr./Ms. (Herr/Frau) to emphasize your respect. You may need to balance between their expected holiday schedule and the workload. You may need to spend a lot longer in meetings than you desire or are used to. You may have to sit down more frequently with some of your subordinates to better understand their motivation and personality. You might have to get used to them returning slightly late from their lunch break. You will need to recognize and appreciate cultural differences and local habits that have roots dating back for decades. If you can accomplish all of these, you will be successful easier, earlier, and in the long term.

 **Chapter Takeaways**

• Corporate culture and its national characteristics are decisive in the environment. Study and understand what type of culture is present in your corporation.

• Identify "the way we do things around here" and start working with the levers that work in that culture. You cannot break the culture; it will break you instead. You must conform and find your way to reach your goals within the cultural framework in multinational companies.

Corporate Mission Possible

Chapter III – Jurassic Park

If you have never worked for a large multinational corporation, you may think the organization, as a whole, is not so important or applicable to the everyday workforce. Surely, there is your boss, his or her boss, and so on and so on. If you are a manager or supervisor, you have subordinates, and they may have subordinates under them as well. You may have experienced a similar chain of command in a small company. However, if you are to enter the corporate world, you may encounter quite a different kind of organizational setup. If your company is acquired by a large multinational, you can bet there will be major changes in the organizational structure, and you should be prepared to find your way in the organizational jungle. Why? Because…

THERE IS A GREAT CHANCE THAT YOU WILL NOW HAVE MORE THAN ONE BOSS!

Large corporations long ago recognized that traditional hierarchies of smaller functional organizations do not work efficiently in a huge company. Thus, they adopted a scheme called a "hybrid," or a "matrix organization." This pattern prefers a prevailing operational hierarchy based on the demands of the business. It ensures that customer demands flow through the organization and are being met in a pragmatic manner, with the least organizational resistance (a common phenomenon in functional organizations). Let us see an example.

You know the different objectives of sales and production. Sales want products available at once, as the customer does. Production wants to produce in large quantities to stock and demands forecast from sales; these forecasts cannot always be given, as customers change their demands too often. The two departments therefore clash heads often, one blaming the other for not meeting customer demands or required results. Sales pushes for frequent production program changes and short lead times, while production requires large stock and resists changing the production schedule to accommodate customer demands, thus increasing lead-time. This is further complicated by the fact that customers are infamous for wanting something that is not in stock and wanting it immediately. In a typical large functional organization, this unsolvable issue decreases the competitiveness and efficiency of the organization.

Alternatively, an organization built around customer demand fosters customer-focused teams, where production serves the sales demand as directly and promptly as physically possible. Production receives information from its salespersons continuously and adapts their planning system accordingly so they are capable of reacting on short notice. Production processes are designed so changes and adaptations are natural, frequent, and part of the system; production runs are as large or small as immediate future customer demand.

In such operational organizations, the role of functional managers is to ensure the methodical leadership, fine-tune processes and operational results, and look after the strategic perspective of the business. You can imagine this as a matrix: operational (daily) business running vertically toward the customer and the functional leadership fine-tuning and controlling the process horizontally, across various customer (product, division) lines.

What does all this mean to you, the new member of such a corporate organization? You will have to get used to inhomogeneous operational teams in which your boss, apart from the customer, serves as a division director. You, as the purchasing manager, will report functionally to the VP of Strategic Procurement or someone of the like. Therefore, you will have two bosses, and herein lies the challenge.

I have worked in various matrix organizations, and it has always been very difficult to find the right communication and the right way to move ahead. As management gurus admit, it is by no means a perfect organization scheme, but it is the most effective for large corporations. People like simple relations: they like to know whom they report to and who reports to them. In this type of organization, you are expected to be more sophisticated. You must allow the corporation to manage its size while remaining relatively effective. You have to work on two lines: the operational and the functional, and of course, these lines have opposing objectives in some cases.

Susan M. was a purchasing manager in the operational unit of our corporation. Operationally, her job was to ensure that materials and services were available for production when needed, at a cost that fell within the budget. Functionally, her objectives were to reach 5 percent price reduction on the annual level, improve working capital (decrease stock and increase payment terms for suppliers), and help strategic procurement implement their low-cost sourcing initiative. The latter required the import of every possible component from China. She was convinced that if she changed most of the components to China sourcing, although she would be in a better position to meet her price reduction targets, her working capital would surely go south. In addition, she would jeopardize production flexibility and lead-times.

Susan understood the need to communicate with caution and to be creative. She set up a balance between immediate and long-term benefits. She chose to source components from China but secured a local backup in case of a delay with the container shipments. She worked hard on obtaining discounts from local suppliers; she convinced them if their prices and products were good enough, she'd had no reason to go to China. By ordering the containers of some components, she fulfilled the corporate strategy of the local sourcing, the most important initiative of her functional boss, the VP of Strategic Procurement. By setting up adequate local backup suppliers, Susan ensured flexibility and short lead-times – a must for her operational unit production department.

Success in a matrix organization depends on the individual's ability to find the balance and communicate properly. With proper explanation, you will be able to defend your actions to

Chapter III - Jurassic Park

both bosses; the important thing is that you find the balance that satisfies both to an acceptable extent. You must understand what the most important aspects are for each and look for a suitable compromise. Both will not be happy without reserves. They will be happy enough, however, to consider you a valuable member of their respected teams.

Working in a matrix organization requires a great deal of maturity in dealing with corporate politics. It is most likely that you will have more than two bosses: other operational and functional members will step into your everyday job and will complicate your decisions with their own needs and agendas. Finance, for example, will shout for improving working capital, and you will probably have to report regularly to them or make comments to the financial organization as to why your targets for the month were not met. Quality control will be stubborn to accept the products from China. Production will complain every day about the delivery timeliness from your suppliers. Nobody will show understanding that some of the delays are caused by the undercapitalization of these suppliers, as that does not leave without answer a delay of payment to them (as required by finance at the end of each quarter to improve working capital). If you delay payment, there might be a risk of shipment delay, as they will not be able to buy some of the components on time.

In spite of the existing corporate strategy that all departments should follow and move concurrently to reach the strategic targets, clashing interests and objectives seem to materialize. We'll talk at length about this in the chapter regarding strategy, but know that in order to succeed in this jungle of different immediate interests of departments, you will have to:

BUILD YOUR HORIZONTAL NETWORK.

Pick up some colleagues in finance, quality, production, and sales. (Remember: we are still at the example of the procurement manager). Your choice of these individuals should reflect your mutual sympathy or at least mutual respect. Show your respect to them in your everyday communication and actions and acknowledge theirs. Be nice to them and help them get what they want and get it on time. I know this is not easy to do, but you must give it your best effort. Small favors and the fact that you support their work will enhance their motivation, and they will enjoy working with you. They will return the favor by lobbying for you with their bosses, especially when your interests seem to clash with the boss's interests.

Middle-level managers and professionals in corporate organizations often complain about the contradictory nature of certain objectives or actions of their superiors. The underlying cause is the above-described matrix organization and a different agenda of individual functional and operational teams. Let us not be naïve: corporate strategy does not reflect in every action. Even the most successful corporate organizations cannot ensure that corporate strategy is implemented on the middle-level management without misunderstanding, contradictory actions, and frustration. The higher we go up in the organization, the overall strategy becomes clearer, but it is also more complicated to draw the balance between the different lines of interest and agendas.

The effect of matrix organization on high-level operational managers is quite specific.

I used to be the division director, the boss of Susan M., the purchasing manager in our corporation. I had a team of managers who helped me reach my operational objectives. In contrast, their respective functional bosses managed half of their time, objectives, and efforts. Susan M. reported also to the VP of Strategic Procurement, the same way the quality manager reported to VP Quality, manager of finance to the VP Finance, etc. My daily frustration originated from the need of juggling the demands of my five to six managers and

Chapter III - Jurassic Park

their functional agendas in an effort to deliver required operational results. I had to balance the working capital requirements of a crazy China sourcing plan with the daily needs of paying suppliers and not remaining overdue. I had to allocate adequate resources to continuous improvement actions (required monthly by the VP Quality and the strategic corporate plan), even during the busiest season of the year, when production barely dealt with all the orders and all available resources were assigned to operational activities. I had to be aware of all tasks of the manager of finance that were decided in a worldwide finance meeting attended only by my manager (they forgot to include me, of course). Additionally, I had to communicate with all of the VPs to keep them informed about the operational progress and support of functional initiatives. The fact that I had my own operational (and actually also functional) boss who inquired about the state of affairs daily and demanded results was the icing on the cake.

How can you handle all this without getting a heart attack every week? Well, there are hundreds of thousands of division directors out there. The author of this book used to be one of them, in fact. Only a few of these suffer the occasional heart attack, and I was fortunately not one of those. We have already discussed appropriate and careful communication, but you also need to win over your subordinates so they will support your efforts and decisions. They have to be closer to you than they are to their other bosses, and you are in a better position as you meet them every day. You must be able to lead, couch, and educate them, giving them direction that will help your operational organization in its everyday life. To make your bosses happy enough is one thing. The other is:

MAKE YOUR SUBORDINATES AS HAPPY AS YOUR BOSSES.

You are there to manage an organization and it is not possible to do that alone in a corporation. Your best allies are your subordinates.

Matrix organizations require mature individuals who are good communicators, are happy to work in a multitasking environment, and are flexible enough to change work scope when necessary. Ad hoc project teams are often formed to execute certain corporate tasks. This is normally above the standard and daily workload, so if you are involved in these, you will likely be working late and will have less time with your family. You may be forced to do some traveling.

Nevertheless, nothing helps your career better than a well-executed project in which you are a key player or leader. Projects have a start and an end, mostly clear objectives, and they are measurable. Compared to the everyday corporate life, the orientation in the project environment may seem easier. Do not be mistaken: Projects in multinational corporations are also organized in a matrix manner, and there can be several team members coming from different operational and functional lines of the organization. This makes the project manager's work as complicated as that of the division manager's in the previous example. Emphasis is put on proper and very frequent communication, persuasion, finding allies, and motivation of the project team members. The project manager can be more assertive and straightforward in his or her leadership: He or she must take care only about the short-term motivation of the team members. With the other stakeholders (members of other teams, cooperation partners of the project, typically finance and IT people) of the project, the project manager will have to play a more sophisticated game: to find out their potential agenda and win them for the personal support of the project.

Chapter III - Jurassic Park

State-owned large corporations are clear indicators of how different agendas can clash at the operational level. The matrix functional side is substituted with the political agenda.

George B., my wife's good friend, was managing a large, state-owned oil company. He was extremely good at it: In three years, he facilitated a turnaround, and the underperforming and losing firm became a healthy, money-making enterprise. After the regular general elections, the new minister of industry called him for a meeting. He prepared his results and plans and was looking forward to the discussion. He was more than surprised that the only thing the minister wanted to know what the extent of his marketing budget was, and if it was possible to take a chunk of that for financing an industrial magazine that was close to the minister's heart and interests. It did not take George too long to turn in his notice, claiming that his strategy did not fit the new government.

In order to succeed in the corporation organization jungle, you will not need a machete and resistance against malaria. Instead, arm yourself with extremely effective communication abilities, understanding of individual motivation, creative thinking to find compromise, and resistance against stress and frustration.

 **Chapter Takeaways**

- Corporations often build and maintain a matrix organization. This difficult web of relationships requires special skills if one is to succeed within it.

49

- You need to seek and find balance between contradictory requirements, agendas, and interests and master proper communication to get your way and meet your goals.

- Build your horizontal network of allies from other departments.

- Strive to not only make your bosses happy, but also your subordinates, who will stand up for you and support you in return.

Chapter IV - Lingo Trap

Chapter IV – Lingo Trap

Evelyn M. applied for a job as an assistant to the commercial director at a large brewery. In the interview, her potential future colleagues tried to entrap her with the following question: "What would you do if the customer complained about the insufficient number of tanks?" Although she was not sure what a "tank" was (though she supposed they were not speaking about missing military vehicles), her improvised communication to the complaining customer obtained her the position she wanted, director of communications.

Unfortunately, not all of us are as clever as my friend Evelyn. If you've never worked in the corporation world before, you must be aware of the jargon – the often-used special words, expressions, phrases, idioms, and abbreviations. Without knowing these, the corporate lingo, you will find yourself lost like a tourist in a foreign-speaking land. For instance, I do not suggest you ask about the meaning of "KPI" (key performance indicator), as it will return raised eyebrows and you will look a complete idiot. In contrast, pretending that you understand will eventually backfire on you. Unfortunately, there are no schools I know of that teach Corporate Slang 101, and it would also be out of the scope of this book to include a dictionary (which would still never fully exhaust all terms for all corporations and industries). My advice is to just spend a little time on Google, read business publications, listen carefully when talking to those who have experience with the lingo, and try to use the jargon in your daily communication to show that you are comfortable in such an environment.

Some of the abbreviations are difficult to find on the Internet. Even early on the job, you very well may receive an e-mail that reads: "There is a reduction in FGI due to increased invoicing to a large customer last month, but this is partially compensated with increase of RM due to the production start of a new product. Nevertheless, in total, our WC is getting better." You may not know the meaning of FGI (finished goods inventory), RM (raw material), and the last sentence is not about improvements in the restroom area: WC stands for working capital. In this case, you are left to guess, left at the mercy of your closest colleagues; believe it or not, they may not make a fool of you if you ask them.

Some of the expressions have become industry standards; they are used everywhere, especially in American/British corporations. Due to the mixed culture of corporations, slang expressions can have different meanings, even in different companies within the same country. Therefore, even if you are a seasoned corporate veteran, you may be surprised by some new expressions or abbreviations that you have never heard before. Rest assured that you won't find every answer on the Internet – and some of the ones you do find may be downright wrong for your corporation or industry. Some corporations even invent their own abbreviations or expressions not used anywhere else. DMA may not refer to "direct marketing association" or "direct memory access," as Google suggests; in your company, it may refer to "detailed management account" (something akin to a P&L of a division – profit and loss statement – used at one of the corporations where I worked).

THERE ARE ALSO DANGEROUS EXPRESSIONS.

If you hear "restructuring," you should start paying attention: This means some part of the corporation is not working optimally, and a reorganization is sure to ensue. This can result in a reduction of the number of employees, change of bosses, and change of procedures. "M&A" should raise a red flag too; it stands for "mergers and acquisitions," and it indicates that there will be strategic initiatives for expansion. Companies are bought for their market and customers or technology. Sometimes, purchasers hope to get some of their people, with the emphasis being on the word "some." Therefore, a "merger" is not just simply the fusion of two companies; after the merger, as we've alluded to already, some positions will be doubled and therefore canceled. This can happen either in the company purchased or in the corporation itself.

You should watch out specifically when you hear "rightsizing." The corporate euphemism for cutting jobs ("downsizing" should be the honest name) aims to express that it is nothing more than adjusting the size of staff to the current size of the business. It is interesting that "rightsizing" is never mentioned in connection with mass recruitment.

If you hear about a "corporate lean program," know that it has nothing to do with your personal diet and physical exercises to lose weight. Instead, it means that your corporation has decided to do only things that bring value to the customer. As a consequence, some of the activities, processes (and therefore, of course, people) will be considered redundant and unnecessary. If this occurs in times of business boom, there is no issue, for the company will likely find use for them elsewhere. However, in crisis times (unfortunately the more frequent example), this means inevitable lay-off.

You should learn the corporate lingo as quickly as possible. It will help you to better orient yourself in the corporation and to fit in as an insider. This is an important part of your integration in the corporation. You do not want to stick out unless it's because of your results!

Chapter Takeaways

• Learn the special abbreviations and expressions used in the corporation. Try using them ASAP to show that you are an insider.

Chapter V - Stretched Sails

Chapter V – Stretched Sails

Do you know the strategy of your corporation? What is the direction of the wind, and where is your destination? Unfortunately, most would have to answer that they have no idea, unless you are a high-level manager. Even in that case, this inside knowledge is not guaranteed. I worked for a corporation as an executive, yet it still took me two years to find out what the corporation was up to from a strategic perspective.

Do not be mistaken by the beautifully framed mission and vision statements on the walls of the hallways and offices. Although these are a way to integrate all employees into the basics of the company strategy, they are not very effective in most corporations. Why? Until the written words manifest themselves in everyday behavior, they will remain as nothing more than a declaration on the wall, not even noticed after a couple of months, except, perhaps, by the cleaning staff who has to dust them.

But why should the corporate strategy be of any interest to you? Well, the higher you are on the ladder, the more important for you it becomes. Even if you are a factory worker in a large corporation, there are some basic things you should know. What is more important for the corporation, quality or short-term profit? This is a critical question that is never asked in such a blunt form; either that, or the answer seems to be trivial. Of course quality is more important. This will be said in official meetings and will be reiterated on whiteboards. At the same time, however, your supervisor will tell you, "Don't you dare stop that production line for one disqualified unit! We have quotas and goals to meet, you know!" So, in fact, for the factory worker, the corporate strategy is not what is on the whiteboard or printed in that fancy-font mission statement on the wall or the front page of your employee handbook that you haven't looked at since the day it was issued to you. The corporate strategy for you is to meet your supervisor's demands.

Corporate strategy is decided at the higher managerial or board level. Corporations use the methodology of "strategy deployment" as a gradual split and delegation of various strategic aspects to the right level of the organization. This methodology – at least in theory – is intended to inform all employees about the strategic consequences at their level of the organization. During this process, managers of every level decide how much of the strategy the next level should be aware of. This process, however, is less than perfect in most cases. When there is no direct communication, the different levels work as filters, and the message may significantly change by the time it reaches the shop floor, much like the message at the end of the telephone game we all played as children, whispering into the next kindergartner's ear.

The other issue is inconsistency between strategy and daily behavior. As in the above example of the supervisor's rush due to pressure for output, quality may falter. If the worker notices this and experiences it often, he or she will learn that output (numbers) are more important than quality. Hence, attention will not be given to the perfection or quality of the product. The focus will be to complete the product as soon as possible so it can be shipped, thus avoiding the scolding yells of the supervisor. You can imagine the long-term results of this: increased customer complaints and decreased customer satisfaction.

If you are in a middle managerial position, you and your team are likely measured against a set of parameters (KPIs). If you are lucky, these parameters will help you to convey the strategic message. For instance, if your targets include decreasing of customer claims, reduction of inventory, reduction of production cost, and on-time delivery to customers, your perception of the strategic priorities are clear: improve quality, improve working capital, increase profitability, and improve customer service. Unfortunately, these targets cannot always be reached simultaneously. As the old saying goes, "I can produce cheap, high quality, and fast – but not all at the same time."

Corporate Mission Possible

One large corporation in the beer industry set new strategic targets: increase market share (sell more) and profit margin (raise prices) at the same time. The sales representatives felt caught between the two. They were forced to approach customers (restaurants, bars, and retail food chains) and bombard them with promotional stuff, telling them about the advantages of the strong brand, as well as technical and marketing support. Customers listened willingly until the moment they realized the significant price increase. Since it was a very price-sensitive market, most of the faithful customers succeeded merely remaining at the same volume, but potential new customers were unwilling to give up their brand in order to support the more expensive one offered by the corporation. Some of the customers decided to swap the corporation's brand to a cheaper one. As a result, the market share decreased, and the price increase did not account for the lost volume. Sales reps were extremely frustrated, as their bonuses were directly connected to sales volume. Not only was the campaign counterproductive for the corporation from a financial standpoint, but it also de-motivated its employees.

Strategy offers a general guideline of where the corporation would like to go. There may be several ways to reach that goal. Different departments may build up their own tactics to reach strategic initiatives. The tactical decision of one department can be just opposite of that in another department. Individually, each method would likely prove beneficial; however, when combined, serious confrontations and fights emerge.

During the annual budgeting process, the financial department wants to challenge all divisions' plans in order to maximize committed revenue and profit, while at the same time minimizing costs. This is completely in line with the corporate strategy. The division director is doing his best to come up with aggressive marketing and sales plans and

Chapter V - Stretched Sails

productivity improvement actions, and he is seriously considering potential cost-saving actions in overheads and operations. Budget discussions reveal a 10 percent gap between the expectations of finance (dictated by the board of directors) and the numbers the division director has come up with. After several hours of fruitless mutual convincing, the CEO makes the blunt decision that the division has to rework its plans to meet the dictated figures.

The division director goes home extremely frustrated, without a clue how to reach such a seemingly impossible requirement. Even after a week of further internal discussions with the division managers, only a marginal 2 percent improvement is all they can come up with. As showing up at the next meeting with such a suggestion would be unacceptable, the director suggests manipulating the figures a little, making more aggressive sales plans, increasing prices, and hoping for a large contract midyear. Of course, nobody is any the wiser where this large contract will come from.

The next budget meeting goes well in the beginning. Finance is satisfied, and high-level expectations are met. Unfortunately, one of the other divisions has a major issue already at the end of the current year. It seems that due to the loss of an ongoing contract, they will have to revise their budget and reduce their numbers. The CEO is screaming, finance is calculating, and somebody shouts, "If they improved so much already, they could easily improve them by another 5 percent, right?" The division director does not believe his ears, but before he can open his mouth, the decision is made, and his numbers are increased by another 5 percent. "You are so smart, guys! You will work it out!" says the CEO.

What would be your options as the division director in this situation? Should you just tell your managers they can kiss their bonuses goodbye because reaching 5 percent more is not realistic and is simply...impossible? Should you resign, knowing these irrational expectations will be the end of you, making your job a living hell? Is it worth it to stay and risk all that stress, only to fail in the end? Should you organize a three-day brainstorming session with your managers and go for it, trying to come up with one good plan amongst all of those beautiful minds? Clearly, at this point, it's a matter of fight or flight. In hindsight, you realize you should have been more cautious and should have honestly presented the numbers, even if they were still some percentage off the expectations. You might have been challenged, but you would have likely given in in the end; certainly you would not have been further challenged to stand up for the lagging division.

Different departments implement strategy daily, each employing different vehemence and tactics. Your sister departments are your competition in getting the exact amount of challenge, supporting the corporate with results, and stretching yourself just to the extent bearable. If you lose this fight, you will drown yourself in a much worse condition, shrinking your chance of success. You will pay dearly for your inexperience: you'll spend a horrible year chasing dream targets, working your backside off, and all to the tune of losing your bonus and your clout and reputation in the end.

My experience shows that panicking is of no use. Until the end of the next year, there are still twelve months to go. If you quit, you will never know if you might have succeeded. Even when the odds seem impossible, you should start working toward something. Sure, you might have made a mistake that you swear you will never make again, but now you must find a way to improve.

My friend, John L., found himself in a similar position. Fortunately, he did not give up. The worldwide economic crisis of late made it painfully clear to all corporate board members that no growth can be expected. Actually, they were happy to except that our division director reached only slightly decreasing numbers instead of significant growth budgeted. Although he did not earn his bonus, he could at least offer some to his team for their efforts, and he came out of that year as a solid manager who is capable of surviving even critical times. He lost the battle, but he eventually won the war: during the next budget process, he was able to enforce a much more cautious approach that resulted in moderate growth. Given his acquired momentum in the business the previous year, he exceeded the following year's budget by a large amount and went home with a spectacular bonus.

Corporate strategies may change, perhaps more frequently than you might expect or appreciate. Major changes in the marketplace can force companies to change their strategies in order to succeed in the new environment. Unfortunately, strategy tends to change even due to personal circumstances on the executive or board level, and of course, when there is a switch in ownership. One year you chase market share, the next profit margin. Another year, the focus will be on growing services. At least this is how the employees – and sometimes among them, unfortunately, middle-level managers – perceive the changes. Rarely are strategy changes communicated properly in corporations at all levels. In most of the cases, no long-term view is given to the middle level, causing a build-up of frustration and confusion.

If your corporation does not communicate properly its reasons for strategy change and its long-term perspectives, you are left to find your own motivation. If you are a middle-level manager, you must find ways to motivate your staff and explain the sudden changes in objectives or direction. Sit down and try to figure out what the story is and how you can explain it. Even if it is not the real story, you have to serve your subordinates a framework that makes sense to them. You must explain the changes, the reasons why, and the tools, skills, and procedures that will be needed to follow the new strategic direction. Revealing your own frustration, cluelessness, and de-motivation will only result in disorientation and lead to certain failure.

One of my fellow managers, excellent communicator Gary Z., executed this properly. His corporation heavily invested in acquisitions in the past years and realized large investments in technology. All of a sudden, investments were seriously cut for the following year's budget, no new acquisitions were allowed, and high expectation to increase profitability was demanded in budget targets. The official communication from the board level explained the change of strategy as shareholders' requirement to increase return of investment of the business. Gary was frustrated and knew such an explanation would not be palatable to his team, as he could not even stomach it himself. Therefore, he invented a story. He pulled the team together and told them very confidentially that the corporation planned to enter the stock market. He explained that past acquisitions were integral to the strategy to increase the size of the business. Now, the following task was to show the potential investors that such businesses could be successfully consolidated and extensive growth could be translated into large profit growth. That would attract market attention and make sure the IPO would be a success.

The team felt exhilarated. They felt they were part of the corporation's secret strategy. They felt the corporation trusted them and needed them to execute that important step to future growth. They bought in and started working on cost-cutting, connecting synergies of different parts of the corporation and came up with tens of creative and new ideas to boost sales and use the new technology to increase profit margin. Together, they committed to a very aggressive budget.

Chapter V - Stretched Sails

Gary learned midyear from an informal conversation with some of the executives that the real reason for the strategy change was far more prosaic. The corporation had lost part of its financing and had to refinance with a different bank, relying on private equity sources. This, of course, caused a sudden lack of cash and the immediate need to milk as many cows as possible. Gary was surprised but allowed his story to continue, as the first results showed very promising. By the end of the year, they beat the budget in terms of profit, and his only task was to figure out how to explain that there were no IPO plans yet on the horizon – not that the team would be interrogative, though, for they were too happy with their healthy bonuses to be annoyed or paranoid about anything. The corporation actually entered the stock market the following year.

So, am I telling you to lie? I don't think of it that way, and neither should you. You have to be creative to help yourself in order to survive critical situations, as your corporation will not always help you. Employees require leadership. They want to know that their corporation is not just roaming the business waters without a clear purpose. You, as a manager, have to deliver this leadership in order to keep motivation up and deliver results. Even if you have to make up your own story as to where the corporation is going. Let the employees feel informed and included, and they will help you get there.

 **Chapter Takeaways**

- Corporate strategy is not always clear, sometimes not even for the board.

- Daily practice is often contradictory to official strategy statements.

- The methods of tactical implementation of strategy differ in all departments. Do not be surprised if you must fight to get your way.

- Do not let yourself be bullied into too-aggressive strategic plans. If you have fallen prey to this, work hard and pray for opportunities that will decrease the pressure.

- If you are not able to find clear strategy, make up one yourself for the sake of your team.

Chapter VI - The Most Powerful Thing

Chapter VI – The Most Powerful Thing

I joined a large manufacturing corporation as a manager in the beginning of my career. My job included materials management, production planning, and procurement. Everyday interaction with the production lines found me frequently in the production hall, and I picked up some data during the process. When the divisional director, frustrated with the insufficient output of the production, paid a visit to our factory, I made some comments about the production output. It turned out that I remembered much more of the numbers than the production manager. Several discussions, an interview, and a month later, I found myself promoted to the newly created position of operations director, heading production, materials, quality, customer service, and human resources.

Knowledge and information becomes an ever-growing currency in our world. Why should this be different in the corporation? Your education and professional experience has equipped you with hard knowledge and soft skills. Based on this, you are a valuable professional; this qualifies you to fill a well-paid job in a corporation. It is, however, only the starting point. How successful you become depends on how much information you are able to gain access to and how creatively you use that information. On the contrary, lacking information is a serious handicap that can be fatal.

One of my most important requests to my subordinates as a corporate director has always been to make sure I receive a copy of all important messages outgoing from our division. It could be a report or just an information transmission; when colleagues are in doubt about my inclusion, I ask them to copy me on it just to be on the safe side. I never complain if I am copied unnecessarily, for pressing the delete button does not take much effort. On the contrary, when I am not kept in the loop on an issue or a report that goes to my superiors or another corporate department, nothing is more embarrassing than receiving a phone call from my boss requesting an explanation on some of the figures or asking for other details that I haven't been made aware of. It is said that "Knowing is half the battle," but I would suggest that it's more valuable than that. Information increases your control and enables you to react properly. A lack of information makes you look like a

Chapter VI - The Most Powerful Thing

complete idiot, or at least an incompetent manager. This is not a very good look at all.

As we discussed before in the chapter about strategy, there are different agendas for different departments in the corporation, so the occasional clash is unavoidable. To prevent finding yourself between the clashing shields, you have to keep your ears and eyes open and read between the lines, particularly in e-mail. Your allies from other departments, those who are willing to provide you with corporate gossip, can be invaluable if you learn how to filter out real information from small talk and rumors.

Thomas C. was a very capable corporate procurement manager. He was tasked with the implementation of low-cost sourcing. He worked hard on China suppliers with the supply chain organization for most of the year of 2008; by autumn, he was prepared to start ordering container-based shipments of components that had already gone through quality approval at headquarters. Fortunately, he was also invited to a budget meeting, and he understood that several divisions had a genuine fear of decreasing sales based on the news about the budding financial crisis. Corporate management was still very optimistic, though, and no change of plans on China sourcing was mentioned. Thomas decided to hold off on the orders to China, making an excuse of a further qualification test that needed to be done. It was a hot situation, as the Supply Chain VP was raving mad; his assumed savings for the next year's budget suffered a big dip. Thomas stood his ground and, building on the strong, high-quality strategy of the corporation that would not allow nonqualified purchases, he succeeded in postponing the order to China by three months. This automatically decreased his savings budget for the next year, and the gap was then transferred to some poor devil of a sales division to take care of. After the three months (January 2009) it was crystal clear that no China orders would be issued for a long time. Sales dropped by 50 percent, and there was enough stock to survive the whole year. Thomas escaped being fired. How? By using information cleverly: If he had ordered the lines of container shipments, he would have been forced to take the blame for the overstock of half a million USD. As a side effect, he had a decreased savings budget that, although with difficulties, he succeeded to meet by the end of 2009. He was one of the few employees in the corporation to receive a bonus that year.

Information circulates nowadays with incredible speed. Although being on a Smartphone or device equipped with e-mail technology can be a pain in the backside, it has its clear advantages. Several times, I captured an e-mail on my Blackberry that would have threatened an international scandal left unattended. An unsatisfied international customer's reaction to an announcement of a late delivery, copied to your superiors, is a serious issue. If you are the manager responsible for the shipping division and you are lucky enough to be copied on this message, inadvertently or otherwise, you have to act very quickly. There is a good chance that you can do something about it. Certainly, you have to contact the customer the same minute and let him know that you will take care of the issue and will find a solution with your team in the following hours. You have to do this before your boss calls you about it so that you can report that you are already handling the matter. Eventually you will find a feasible solution that will satisfy the customer; perhaps you can provide better delivery time. The most important thing is having the information that something is amiss and jumping to solve it ASAP.

Information may trigger actions, or it may be kept to oneself. Corporations often filter information to lower levels of management. In the chapter about strategy, I talked about the situation when the refinancing plans of the corporation were not released, even to responsible managers. In case of my

Chapter VI - The Most Powerful Thing

friend Gary Z., this caused lack of information that he filled in with a story to keep team motivation high. Should the corporation have communicated the news of refinancing to him? Although it would have been fair, I am not sure it would have been clever. News about the need for refinancing could have caused panic. The ugly thing is, lack of information can cause an even bigger panic and leaves room for assumption, gossip, and speculation. If you are in a position to fill in the gap with positive information, do it. You may not have all the facts, but it's still better than letting employees fill it themselves.

As a corporate manager, you will experience numerous situations when information provided to you will be confidential. Never break your word in order to release it to somebody. Knowing about something gives you power, as you can think about your actions and be sure they will be better aligned and more successful. If your superiors know you are trustworthy, they will provide you with more and more confidential information that will only strengthen your position.

From a moral perspective, there are issues, that can be difficult to solve. I've experienced more of these than my fair share.

I used to manage a manufacturing plant of a corporation, more than a decade ago. The company headquarters decided to consolidate manufacturing facilities in crisis time, and my plant was up for closure. Manufacturing would be transferred to some low-cost country. I was aware that the decision would be communicated in a week. One of my managers, a good friend who had only joined the corporation some time before, had been contemplating settling in our city with his family, to put an end to his fifty-mile daily commute. He wanted to buy a home in the vicinity and was on the verge of signing the mortgage papers. As he had seen some signs that things had not been going well, he asked me for advice as

69

to whether or not he should buy the property and relocate his family. Naturally, I could not reveal to him what I knew, so I told him to wait one week before he signed anything. Still, I felt it was not the best advice, and I feared he might suffer some financial loss because he had to make a down payment, but I simply could not tell him more. I could not tell him, "For Christ's sake, do not buy a property here. In three months you will not have a job, or at least not in this town."

After the week, he learned the news and canceled the agreement. He did not sign the full contract and the mortgage papers, so his loss was minimal, but it was a loss nonetheless. I am sure he was very angry with me at the time, but a savvy businessman in his own right, he later understood that I did not have an option.

There are people in corporations who know very well the power of information and take advantage of it. I believe in knowledge and talent. I believe both should form the foundation of your corporate career and not the information you gather and take advantage of. Nevertheless, I also believe it is all right to

USE INFORMATION TO ENHANCE YOUR KNOWLEDGE AND TALENT

BUT NOT TO SUBSTITUTE FOR THOSE.

A's select A's into their team. B's select C's and D's. B's build their power on the information they are hoping to gather in their position and select less-capable subordinates who cannot challenge them. Some corporations are full of such managers and team leaders. It is your choice to decide in what category you belong and what the best path is for you.

Most corporations realize they do not have all capabilities they need for their strategy execution. Instead of trying to find employees with the right knowledge, they hire ad hoc consultants as the need arises. External consultants work on a

Chapter VI - The Most Powerful Thing

well-defined project, making good use of their own knowledge and "external" information, but they cannot work without the internal information necessary for the successful project execution. They put great effort into acquiring that internal information from employees. During this process, employees often recognize them or their project as a threat to their own position, structure, or personal objectives.

I used to work as an external consultant for some years for middle and large corporations, implementing certain processes and introducing change. Some of the employees caused me headaches, as they justified their way of doing things by deliberately refusing to share vital information. Although it is understandable self-defense, it is seldom successful. The clever consultant finds a way to collect the information needed. The employee who chooses to withhold information will not be in a position to discuss the findings, since he or she was not cooperative and will, therefore, be dismissed from potential discussions. It should also be noted that uncooperative employees do not last long in an ever-changing environment.

You can build your future position only with a cooperating attitude. Remember that it is not only about what you are doing that counts in the corporation. It is about what you can do for the company you represent. Your potential, especially in time of change, will decide if your career will continue – in that corporation, in another, or at all.

Chapter Takeaways

• Stay in the loop! Be sure you are copied on all e-mails connected to your area of operation. It is no harm for

you to be copied more than necessary, but missing one e-mail that you should have been copied on can be fatal.

- Listen to and filter corporate gossip to be on point on important matters.

- If you discover pertinent information about urgent issues, react on issues before your superior tells you to.

- Never release confidential information to anyone.

- Remember that information cannot replace your talent and knowledge; it only enhances your ability to use them. .

- Be careful with deliberately withholding information from peers, bosses or consultants, for this can easily backfire. Supply information to your subordinates, even if you don't know all the facts.

Chapter VII – Counting the Beans

Long-term financial results are the driver of success in every business; this is quite commonplace. What is more interesting is that in large corporations, on the level of most employees, monthly and quarterly results gain specific importance.

In most corporations, monthly closures must be reported only a few days after the calendar month end. Quarterly results, especially in public corporations (whose stock you can buy or sell on the stock exchange), are reported publicly, and these have serious effect on the evaluation of the stock. If results are lower than expected (i.e. forecasts the company reported earlier), the stock can decrease by much more than the real gap would indicate: the market reacts in a volatile way to show distrust in a company that is not able to keep its promises. If results are even a tiny bit higher than expected, stock value may increase, and more of it can be sold, given that there will be positive trust in the company's future results.

This is why, in most corporations, publicly reported in-year results have such an importance and focus. This is why your director beats you up every month to meet and exceed the forecast of sales, deliveries, costs, and finally, the profit of the company.

THE BOARD AND THE SHAREHOLDERS ARE NOT INTERESTED IN YOUR PROBLEMS

with competitors, suppliers, employees, or technology; they want their numbers met every month, every quarter, every year.

The critical assumption for success in reaching results – above and in addition to the trivial day-to-day operations – includes thoughtful budgeting (annual assumptions for revenues and costs) and forecasting (monthly and quarterly preview of future status). In the last chapter, we mentioned how my corporate procurement manager friend was able to force down budget savings expectations based on delayed low-cost sourcing shipments. It is critical that you actively take part in the budget and establish a realistic estimate of what is going to happen next year. Even if you are not a director, not directly responsible for the P&L, you should try to provide accurate and cautious estimates from your own field, in terms of costs and revenues. A mistake in a budget (mistakes are always underestimation of costs and overestimation of revenues, never the opposite) can wreak havoc the following year in terms of results, stress, and lost bonuses – and sometimes even worse.

Chapter VII - Counting the Beans

Of course the corporation will want you to grow 20 percent next year, all while increasing productivity and profitability. In other words, the dreamers that they are, they want you to do it without hiring anybody. During the budget meetings, you or your superiors will fight with corporate executives about a reasonable compromise. This is the most difficult period of the year. You must have many underlying figures, analysis, and arguments to back up your claims and defend your position. You must be prepared to answer every possible question. Your plan must be logical and reasonable, with no holes or gaps, and hard data must support your assumptions, if possible.

The recipe for a realistic budget is as follows: one-part good preparation and one-part even better luck. Even if you have the best preparation in the world, you likely cannot tell the future; few executives carry crystal balls in their briefcases. Your assumptions, therefore, must remain on the cautious side. Be prepared for battle, my friend, for the corporation will challenge you on each and every one of them. Your superiors will push you to grow more than you would like. They will expect to save costs and at the same time push for higher performance. They will expect you to be as aggressive as they are, if not more so. You will have to use all your brains and negotiation skills to present and defend a budget that looks aggressive enough without being completely impossible.

THE SECRET IS IN BUILT-IN CONTINGENCIES.

Let us say there is a strategic product line where above-average growth is expected. You will have to show very aggressive plans here, even if you are not so confident; otherwise, your budget will be swept off the table. On the other hand, another product line may have higher possibilities but less focus. Here, you should budget an average growth and make realistic plans behind the curtains, ensuring a contingency. You should be prepared to defend your cost base, even if you know you could save a couple of dollars here and there. If you strip all your resources away, there will be no contingencies to turn to if things go worse than budgeted.

ONCE YOUR BUDGET IS APPROVED, YOU ARE LOCKED IN.

Corporations do not like to change their budgets midyear, even if market changes indicate that they should. In-year changes materialize in forecasts that, in the best case, copy or exceed budget; in the worst case, these assume lower results than budget. This is already bad news, and it will be fought against with vehemence and much vigor by your superiors, who are always looking at the bottom line.

You have a chance to play with your (monthly, quarterly) forecasts against your budget several times during the year. You cannot afford to accept a budget in December and then make your January forecast showing a decrease in your annual results below budget, even if market conditions changed. You must stick to the budget for several months, indicating that you have the energy and the results to help you fight, even in the worst of conditions. Things can change during the year, so there is no rush to admit defeat in the beginning. If you are able to win a couple of battles early on, you will build trust, and your superiors will know that you will strive to do your best. Only if you consume all of your contingencies and keep your results – although barely – on budget level in the first part of the year should you then try to submit a forecast in the middle of the year that might show some deterioration from the budget, if this is necessary.

Willy F., my clever friend, has been managing a construction division of a corporation. His budget was set with double-digit annual growth and typical gradual increase of revenues that culminated in the season of summer months. He did not have problem meeting first-quarter revenues and profits, as these were mild, out-of-season numbers. The problems started with the second-quarter growth, which was showing behind-budget results. The market was slow, and there were no new large projects to build. As soon as he realized that he would miss the budget without those new projects, both on revenue and profit, he started to reinforce his contingency plan: He used the purchasing power and cash of his company to get construction material cheap on stock and sell it to small, private builders with discount. This business activity could be operated with much less direct workforce than real constructions, so he saved some on workforce and did not have to hire temporary workers. The buy-and-sell operation of construction materials showed success among the small builders. It supplied less revenue than the big projects but still turned in a healthy profit margin. This, in combination with the workforce cost savings, substituted the gap of profit from the missing large projects, and my friend survived the summer. He actually was doing better than the budget, but he left some reserves every month in the balance sheet "for potential material quality claims." A good return policy with his suppliers allowed him to have no cost on quality claims, so these reserves served also as a contingency. During autumn and winter, he was able to release these reserves and improve his last-quarter results, allowing him to close the year with a tiny profit above budget. He was the hero of the year for the corporation.

There is no need to release better-than-budgeted results during the year. If you have a good month, find legitimate reasons to build reserves for worse months ahead.

THERE IS ALWAYS A REASON TO PUT UP RESERVES:

accruals for potential claims or repairs, underestimated costs (missing invoices), bad debts, accruals for larger-than-budgeted marketing costs in the coming months, etc. All of this is acceptable and legal. If you build up your pillow, you'll sleep more soundly. If things take a downturn, you can reevaluate the necessity of these reserves, and you may decide to release them. You can support your bottom line in a not-so-good month, still meeting budgeted profit in the long run.

Corporations do not like spiking results. Actually, they like all spikes above budget but hate negative spikes, of course. It is much more acceptable for you to meet your budget and your forecast every month, no questions asked. If you are not able to make reserves for some reason or the above-budget profit is too high and you have to admit some of it in the results, you should consider smoothing your next forecast. If you leave your next months on the budget level and do not decrease them a little, your annual profit will be above budget; if this happens, there is no way back. In a couple months, you may experience some bad market changes that will decrease your revenues and profit below budget level, and you will have to forecast decreasing profit. This is bad news.

NO SENSE CHEERING ONE MONTH

AND CRYING THE OTHER,

FOR IT IS MUCH BETTER TO SMILE EVERY MONTH.

This point is very important. You should start forecasting better annual profit than budget only when you are 100 percent sure you can keep it throughout the end of the year. Your built-up reserves can help make it a sure thing.

Another important use of the built-up reserves is as follows:.

GOOD RESULTS ARE SOMETIMES UNREAL.

Not all corporations have a bulletproof system that prevents human mistakes. Forgotten invoices on real costs, wrong booking of some costs or revenues in the accounting department, booked revenue that next month will have to be fully or partially credited, and false material variances during an inventory check are all reasons for better-than-expected results. You should be very careful when it comes to these faux high hopes! If your results are better than you expected one month, and there is no real explanation for it, make reserves for unaccounted costs. I saved my results several times this way. In almost all cases, the better results were not real: one of the above played a role that could not be found during the month-end closing process. This gives you just a couple hours or perhaps a day to challenge your results from the accounting department. The investigations during the next month and the month-end closure itself always cleared up and returned the results. Can you imagine what would happen if your profit one month is $30,000 higher than the budgeted $100,000 and you leave it as it is? Your annual profit expectation immediately increases by this $30,000 unless you modify down your forecast. The following month, your results will be $70,000 instead of the budgeted $100,000, due to the reversal of the mistake that caused the $30,000 better results last month. Not only will you have a real hard time explaining the sudden dip in the month, but also you will have to downgrade your annual forecast by $30,000 on profit. If your corporation is a public company, downgrading the forecast can be very damaging to the stock price. Your issue will go to the board, and you can rest assured there will be visits, including one or more from the boss or bosses of your boss. You will become the focus of intense investigations by the corporation, keeping you from doing your work. They will ask you to report this and that, they will scrutinize your division and operations. There will be a million questions to contend with, and you will not have all the answers. Why risk this if you can prevent it?

In large public corporations, monthly financial closures are a very stressful period. You have three to four days for basic P&Ls (divisions, factories, companies) to close the month and report your results. This is normally not enough to receive all the invoices from the suppliers and consolidate all costs against revenues. The general practice is to make accruals on all costs that can be expected and estimated. The monthly accruals are then released next month, invoices are booked, and new accruals are generated. Although this process is complicated (lot of work for the financial department), it is the only way to report results in that meager window of time. Also, this is a great help in your monthly forecasts, if you take all the accruals into consideration.

In our post-Enron times, corporations are very careful with their accounting. Bookkeeping and managerial processes are subject to strict control. Nevertheless, none of the above processes or advice is illegitimate. It is only common sense, and in the intention of post-Enron policies, not to paint a better picture about the company until it is proven and sure. What you cannot do is use this advice across the end of the fiscal year. At the end of the year, you should clear your balance sheet and leave only reserves that will stand the scrutiny of the most eagle-eyed auditors. These could be reserves for bad debts, accruals for bonuses for the past year (to be paid after the year is audited), or reserves for reasonable costs connected to future quality claims during the warranty period. Do not include reserves for potential non-booked invoices or accruals for potential overestimated revenues or suspicious material variances, for these have to be solved during the year. Leaving unrealistic reserves for bad debts or for future quality claims with the intention of moving some of the profit to next year can be considered tax evasion, a criminal act. Your auditors will make sure this does not happen. Fortunately, if you are a P&L owner, it is in your best interest to maximize the profit for the year, as this is the basis for your bonus.

Chapter Takeaways

• Do whatever you can to meet forecasts. Corporations and their stockholders do not like negative surprises.

• A mistake in the budget is fatal. Resist the pressure to put too-optimistic numbers in budget.

• Whenever you do better than expected, think of worse times ahead and make reserves. They will come handy. Smooth month-by-month results build confidence.

• Operate your finances within legal limits. Clean your balance sheet at the end of the year according to auditors' advice and maximize your annual bonus.

Corporate Mission Possible

Chapter VIII – Answer the Question

Maybe you think nothing is easier than to communicate. After all, you do it every day, constantly, with everyone you come into contact with: family, colleagues, bosses, subordinates, the authorities, friends, the grocer, the bartender, and so on. With some, you talk personally. Sometimes you have to phone, or maybe you are forced to write a letter or drop a quick e-mail. There is even the nonverbal communication your body performs when you interact with others. Communication is as common as breathing, walking, and eating. And by the way, have you noticed what the media has been telling us nowadays about not eating properly? Surely one would think that eating, a basic activity in life, would be something everyone can do properly! It's simple really. You take a nice steak, medium, with some salad and tasty roasted potatoes, make the right cut with the knife, help with the fork, open your mouth, put it in, chew, swallow, and that's that. But now you must think about the ingredients, their origin, and the way of preparation. You must consider the additives, timing, frequency, quantity, and who knows what else.

Truthfully, it is very similar with communication. It may seem trivial, a given, to greet the bank assistant differently than your boss. Sometimes a phone call is more effective and desirable than a text message or e-mail. You certainly do not want to share sensitive or highly confidential information electronically, as such should be handled face to face. As we've mentioned, you will speak differently to the people on the shop floor and the CEO of your company and the customers you communicate with.

EFFECTIVE COMMUNICATION WILL BE A KEY TO YOUR SUCCESS IN THE CORPORATION.

When it comes to communication in the corporate environment, there are many opportunities to fail. Due to the importance of presenting yourself and your results, building an image and position, proper communication is part of the toolbox that will help you succeed. You should not underestimate the effects of this on how colleagues, subordinates, or bosses in the corporate body will perceive you and your results. Nevertheless, suboptimal communication is a daily mistake made by even high-level managers in corporations and can lead to fatal consequences.

Most of us are quite inexperienced in choosing the proper way to communicate a message clearly, without distortion. This is

Chapter VIII - Answer the Question

even more difficult if your communication is part of a plan to reach your objectives and needs to be sophisticated in a multi-auditor environment, as e-mails are, with their copy possibilities.

We sit in front of our computers or hold our Blackberries, iPads, or Smartphones, reading and sending e-mails and text messages all the time, often without a second thought. It frequently happens that the chain of e-mails become a heated conversation, a feast of arguments. I have been copied on some nasty conversations between my subordinates from different departments or arguments between divisions, electronic discussions in which strong language – much too strong for a professional setting – was used. This is unacceptable in most corporate environments. My advice is to always handle disagreements in person, or at least on the phone. The written words, with their directness and potential longevity (those e-mails may remain in somebody's inbox or other directory for much longer than you anticipate), have a dangerous nature. Also, without the inflection of voice or facial expression to accompany them and convey emotion, they can be perceived as harsher than they were probably originally intended. They can poison relationships for a long time. Having a discussion or even a heated argument about the same topic in person, on the other hand, offers the advantage of exchange and emotional conveyance, immediate actions and reactions, and body language that can help each to interpret the intention properly.

One of my subordinates answered a colleague without even addressing her by name: "No need to send me reminders every day. I have the thing under control." He may as well have said, "Look here, missy...leave me alone!" Although I understand the frustration of getting a repeated e-mail reminder, it does not justify a rude answer. If you get an e-mail that angers you, do not answer it on the spot – especially if it is from your boss. Go for a cigarette or have a coffee, take a walk in the office, wait until lunchtime, or do anything that will give you some time to digest the words, think them over, and answer appropriately. After you've had time to think it over, it's best to pick up the phone and take care of the matter that way.

As a general rule, do not answer confrontational e-mails immediately. Collect yourself, get your argument together, and think it over. If you have to react in an e-mail, choose your words properly so you will address the problem and not personally attack the sender. Too many employees lose their jobs because they are unable to control their emotions. Putting your emotions into a written proof is not very clever; it will turn against you eventually.

Even when talking face to face, you should carefully choose your words. One of my colleagues, an emotional talker, likes using the argument, "This is not true." His opponents might interpret this as him saying, "That is a lie!" or "You're such a liar!" If he encounters someone who is as emotional as he is, which does sometimes occur, they may lose control and will not be willing to discuss things reasonably and rationally. At that point, the discussion will go nowhere. Always try to envision and hear your communication through the eyes and ears of the one you are speaking to. I again emphasize that it is not important what you wanted to say; it is important what the other party heard or understood. Instead of calling him a liar, you could say something like, "I think there is a different way to look at this," or "Well, from another perspective..." The objective of the discussion is never to abuse or prove the other party wrong. Instead, you should be working toward a mutually acceptable solution. This, of course, requires training, the taming of your ego, and certain humility. It is not the other person you are trying to win over; you should be focused on being victorious over the problem you are both trying to solve.

Chapter VIII - Answer the Question

Let us revisit the idea of e-mail again. These quick electronic messages can be a very complicated means of communication, for they may be seen by many eyes besides the main person to whom you are sending them. You can choose to answer an e-mail that was sent to you and several people at least four ways:

1. Public discussion. If you press the "answer to all" or "reply to all" button, your response will be sent to everyone who received the original e-mail. You can use this option to deliver important information to all participants. This is a very useful way to keep many people in the loop, without necessarily asking them to respond or react. All stakeholders in the project or matter in question should be copied on responses to the issue.

2. Extended discussion. Similar to a public discussion, you will copy everyone who received the original message, but you can also extend the copy to additional persons who might benefit from being involved in the conversation. Typically, you can use this when you want other people to be aware that something is going on. For instance, maybe you want to let your boss know about a specific issue. You may also decide that the matter requires a broader audience than was originally considered.

3. Internal discussion. You may decide that your answer or response should not be a matter of public discussion, but only sent to carefully selected persons from the original list. Typically, you will use this option if the e-mail went to a large group of people, but before you respond to everyone, you have a matter to discuss with only one or a few. In this case, you copy only the people in your own organization who are relevant to the matter; after the resolution is clear internally, you can communicate the result to the whole group.

4. Private discussion. In most e-mail software or applications, if you press the "answer" or "reply" button, you will be replying only to the person who sent the message to you. Perhaps you want to discuss the matter with the person in private or you want to provide comments and feedback, suggest some modifications to the topic, or instruct the sender before others are involved.

5. Passing the message. You can press the "forward" button and send the message on to others who were not originally copied, just so they will be aware that such a message is being passed around. This can be used to keep pertinent people informed about things they should be aware of.

Typical and frequent mistakes are made when these forms of handling the message are inadvertently mixed up. I always request from my subordinates that they use "reply to all," unless they have a good reason not to. As I've mentioned before, it is far worse to go uninformed than to be over-informed and receive copies of things I already know about. Nothing is more frustrating than being informed of the first thread of a discussion or a problem, then being left out, just to find out later that the matter was not handled properly. In most of these cases, the issue grows to a serious problem without the superior's knowledge, only to boomerang back on the unsuspecting manager later – in the worst case, your boss finds out before you do. Keeping everyone involved in the entire thread of conversation gives you a chance to steer the issue before it becomes a real problem.

Say a customer sends a request to your sales manager on Tuesday and copies you on it. You make a mental or physical note that something is going on and decide to monitor the answer. On Thursday, you still do not see any answer, but all of a sudden, your boss calls, demanding to know why you are not serving that important customer well, for they've just called him to complain about the solution being offered by your sales manager. You storm out of your office to find the sales guy and demand an explanation. He tells you that he discussed the matter with the suppliers, and they informed

Chapter VIII - Answer the Question

him that there are difficulties with the lead-time. You know about none of this, of course, because he forgot to copy you. Now you have phone calls to make, first to the customer to apologize and promise to find a solution. Furthermore, you will have to organize calls with the procurement, calls to different suppliers, and a final call to the customer to keep them abreast of what's going on. Finally, you call or e-mail to your angry boss to let him know the matter has been solved to the satisfaction of the customer.

All of this inefficiency, embarrassment, and potential damage to the company reputation results from a simple human mistake in communication. Thus, use the "answer to all" button in all cases, unless you have a specific reason not to. The specific reason in the above case might have been that you had wanted to make sure your sales manager handled the important customer request properly. You should have answered to him only, "Be careful. This is an important customer. Do whatever we need to do to meet his request." Such a statement could have increased his focus and most probably would have prevented him from giving the customer a suboptimal solution.

Copying your boss on all e-mails does have its limitations, however. For instance, you would not want to copy your boss just to sponge off his or her power in a dispute with somebody in the department or in another department. If you take this route, you will, in essence, be transferring responsibility, admitting that you are not able to solve the issue yourself. Bosses do not like this hidden way of involving them in your issues, especially if you make them responsible for your actions.

Using corporate e-mail for private matters is also frowned upon in most corporations. Your employer may monitor your e-mail (actually, they are legally entitled to monitor anything you do on your corporate computer). In most cases, the corporate code of ethics states that private use of corporate e-mail is regulated. (Learn more about the corporate code of ethics in the next chapter). You should be aware of these rules, and I suggest adhering to them. After all, you are being paid to accomplish company business in the workplace, not to chat with your friends and family.

An e-mail with the following text appeared in all e-mail inboxes in a middle-sized corporation: "I have kittens for sale. Please contact me if you are interested." The poor sender used some of the pre-created groups in the e-mail program, including all and every member of the organization, counting over 1,000 addressees. After she received a warning from her boss about the e-mail, which clearly violated corporate communication standards, she sent the following message: "I apologize for this e-mail." Of course, she again sent it to all in the corporation...

Some e-mail threads can be superfluous. Instead of ten e-mails going back and forth between two colleagues who sit in the next office to each other, they should just meet in person, discuss, and solve the matter in a five-minute conversation. Even more embarrassing is when this thread has ten other members of the organization copied. If you can, just step in and ask them to get it offline, call each other, or sit down and have a talk.

Conference calls are a special communication method that is used very commonly in large corporations. They can be very efficient for connecting smaller groups without anyone needing to physically be in the same place at once. Do not be surprised if you are invited to several conference calls on different topics daily if you work for a large corporation. Do not hesitate to utilize this method of communication, especially if there is a problem that will be better handled interactively than via an e-mail chain among various groups of employees. As in any other meeting, they should be well prepared, with an agenda, so that time will not be wasted and only matters of benefit and interest to all parties will be discussed. Follow-up of conference calls is as important as the call itself, so never let the call simply go forgotten. A written summary of the takeaways and follow-up actions should be circulated by e-mail to all participants after the call.

In-person conversations tend to be uncommon in our modern digital world. Even personal appraisals are done via widespread computer networks, through e-mails and telephone and filling in forms rather than in person. Still, do not underestimate the importance of sitting down once in a while with your colleagues, boss, or subordinates for a face-to-face conversation, which will allow you to solve many issues and make sure you're all on the same page.

Combining different methods of communication and using them appropriately and effectively is an important tool of success. Not only will this provide pure operational results, but it will also help you properly understand what the important issues are and find the right paths between and among humans to solve them.

Chapter Takeaways

• Choose your ways and means of communication carefully, depending on the situation and your communication partner.

• It is not important what information you wanted to transmit; it is important what your communication partner understood.

- Adhere to specific rules in e-mail communication. Never answer an e-mail when in anger. Cool down, think it through, and answer intelligently and proactively.

- Do not use corporate e-mail for private communication.

- Do not use e-mail when a phone call or in-person talk would be more effective or in serious disputes.

Chapter IX – Rights & Wrongs

Why should ethical behavior be different in the corporate world from the world outside those office doors? Should you behave differently from nine to five than you do after or before work?

A corporate code of ethics or code of conduct sets the legal, moral, and professional rules under which the corporation and its employees should work. It should be your Bible, your law. In large corporations, this can be a very lengthy document; as a corporate employee, you should read and sign off, stating that you will adhere.

There are several reasons for the existence of corporate codes of ethics, especially in large organizations. The general law and generally accepted moral standards are not specific enough to ensure that every employee will behave according to rules that help the corporation reach their mission and be successful. The corporate codes of ethics are also connected to the corporate social responsibility, a self-regulatory policy how the corporation monitors, controls, and ensures the positive effect of its business to the world, including environment and society.

Especially in large multinational corporations, the rules set in codes of ethics are stricter than those of the countries in which the corporation is active. The reason is obvious: setting more demanding rules can minimize the risk that corporate behavior (as a result of accumulated behavior of its employees) will violate the law. This naturally causes conflicts with employees who have difficulty understanding the necessity for stricture rules.

I had been managing a manufacturing company acquired by a large corporation. New safety rules were introduced on the shop floor, including the constant wear of safety glasses. Warehouse employees sitting on a section of the shop floor in an open warehouse complained about the required safety glasses. They sat in front of computers to book in and out material, registering transactions, and they did not see the benefit of wearing safety glasses, as no arbitrary steel chip could fly out of a computer screen to damage their eyes, as was the case for the CNC machines some 200 feet away. In the beginning, I understood their reasoning and allowed to the store employees to go without the glasses while sitting at their computers. This, however, served as an excuse for other employees to take off their glasses whenever they were not working directly at a lathe. Discipline was gone, and there was a real danger for some of the employees who did not want to wear their glasses, even when they should have. I had to put a stop to it, and the next Monday, the strict safety glasses rule was reapplied. The glasses were to be worn everywhere on the shop floor, without exception. Anyone who refused to comply was threatened with a fifty-dollar fine. Several months of grunting followed, but after a year, nobody ever mentioned the matter again, and it became part of the company standard. We never had an eye injury during the two years I served there.

Charlie S. used to work for a large brewery in Europe. Their premium product was traditionally connected in the country with consummation for special occasions, especially for Christmas. One year, in the framework of a pre-Christmas communication campaign, Christmas symbols were used in the media, namely the three wise men and the Star of Bethlehem. Some religious customers complained about the use of these symbols for commercial purposes, especially in marketing alcoholic drink. The media created a huge fuss (as the media seems to enjoy doing), resulting in a damaged reputation for the company. The brewery decided to draw up very strict rules for marketing communication in the future. Before the following Christmas, connecting the premium beer with its historical background, marketing came up with a colored stained-glass motive to be used in the communication campaign. Despite the results of the marketing research being excellent before that campaign, after serious internal discussions, the idea of using the stained-glass was dropped, as it too much resembled the windows common to Catholic and other churches. Many marketing employees were shocked that such a beautiful idea was not okayed by the corporate decision-makers. However, they had their internal rules based on the prior faux pas, and they didn't want a repeat of the same to douse anyone's holiday spirits.

Everyday business reality and a corporate code of ethics can clash very frequently. How do you behave when the rules explicitly prohibit relevant employees having a business lunch with suppliers or customers from time to time? In the old Europe, especially in traditional businesses, relationships are forged over years and include trust and mutual visits above the framework of business. If your company has always given a Christmas present to the major customers in the form of a bottle of wine or some personal item, what will you do when an acquisition by a large multinational corporation forbids these practices, based on a new code of ethics? There are few clever examples to find ways around this. Some salespeople try to manage the business lunch from personal funds, in the belief that the good relationship and the fruitful business will support them in the form of bonuses anyway. You have to understand that the line between corrupt behavior and personal relationships cannot be strictly drawn from the corporate perspective. It is safer to ban presents than to allow them.

Despite the code of ethics, there are numerous examples of rules being bent to fight competition, meet customer needs and requests, and get the results as required. We are not talking about illegal behavior here. Most of these acts happen as a consensus between employees who believe that in the specific situation, the code of ethics of the corporation is superfluous. You have to be careful though: the responsibility for the act remains with you. Your boss might ask you to complete a transaction that may violate the code of ethics, even if it is not illegal. You should be clever enough to refuse this without annoying your superior. This is one of the most difficult situations to handle, and it is a personal choice that you may have to make alone.

One difficult part of the code of ethics is harassment in general, sexist behavior in particular. We do not want to discuss here the trivial examples of sexual or other harassment

Chapter IX - Rights & Wrongs

or hostile sexism. It is rather the so-called "benevolent sexism" that should be discussed, as its judgment is often ambiguous. In most American corporations, this is a sensitive matter, and rules tend to be strict. In contrast, in continental Europe, we are far more "benevolent."

Being a male, I might have a distorted opinion. I believe in the equality of genders and the merits and talent of the individual. In addition, I also believe in the European cultural heritage and behavioral standards. I try to be chivalrous and open the door for a lady, help with heavy items, or offer a seat – not because I consider her weak or that she needs to be protected, but purely out of kindness and affection.

If there are strict rules in your corporation not to use sexist behavior and you are in a European or Asian subsidiary, be careful opening doors or pulling out chairs for your female colleagues arriving for a visit from the U.S. This does not happen in Japan, anyway. Nevertheless, keep your healthy chivalrous manner to your local women, without being overprotective. Be natural.

My friend, Katja H., worked as a local communication director in a European country in a large multinational corporation. They had a female visitor from the U.S. who had been conducting a communication audit throughout the organization. My friend showed her presentation slides about different areas of marketing activities, communication to VIP customers, and specific promotional events. The auditor was very happy and enthusiastic about the excellent work. One of these promotions was a Formula 1 sponsorship. Among the pictures she also showed one of the female employees who tried to get into the jumpsuit of the contestants. She was mildly overweight, so she struggled with zipping the front, smiling about it in the picture. It was funny to everyone in the room except for the auditor. Her smile froze, and she stopped the praising comments immediately. After that slide, her demeanor completely changed. Fortunately, there was no sensible follow-up after that presentation, but my friend understood that her small joke was not perceived as she'd intended. The auditor considered it a humiliation of the female employee, a sexist joke. Although the joke was completely acceptable in Europe, in corporate America, it caused serious problems.

Make sure that your communication and behavior is always respectful wherever you are, if you want to keep your career.

Chapter Takeaways

• A corporate code of ethics or other rules, especially safety, are stricter than legally binding rules. This allows the corporation enough space not to get into trouble with the law.

• Exceptions weaken the rules and soften discipline. It is not worth it, even if rules seem to be too strict.

• Never let yourself be bullied into an act against the code of ethics, even if your superior asks you to do so. You will risk being fired.

• Sexist behavior or jokes are forbidden in American corporations. Observe the culture and adjust your behavior to prevent issues with benevolent sexism – not to mention outright harassment.

Chapter X – Climbing the Ladder

A corporate career is very attractive to most of the corporate employees. Why would so many work there otherwise? Young employees join corporations with high ambitions and a clear target to succeed and step up the corporate ladder and retire as a VP or a CEO. They are willing to put into their dream a lot of work and energy. Unfortunately, many end up leaving much earlier, without ever reaching their original goal. The sad thing is, if you fail on a certain step of the ladder, you cannot just step back on. In most of the cases, you fall all the way down and have to start all over again. . .

Jan K. was a promising and ambitious country manager in a European country of our multinational corporation. He did an excellent job establishing the business in the country, built a solid team, and was highly recognized by the management. He applied for an internal position in the States to manage one of the main subsidiaries of the corporation. He tried to use the same management methods he'd used in Europe and approached the new position with an "I'll show you how to do business" kind of attitude. Within a couple months, it was evident that his new team would not accept him, and he was not able to adapt to the new job environment. In the meantime, his former job was filled by another internal candidate. Thus, his career in that corporation came to a sad end.

There is nothing wrong with being ambitious. Lofty goals trigger high motivation and performance. Nonetheless, I have demonstrated in previous chapters that performance is just one necessary, albeit unsatisfactory, requirement to success in the corporate world. Your whole personality, your communication and presentation abilities, your mental and verbal capabilities, your adaptability and tolerance toward corporate behavior, and eventually your luck will all play a role in how far up the ladder you can go.

We are all constantly learning during our journey, constantly building our career. We learn new skills, sharpen and fine-tune some old ones, learn how to eliminate unwanted behavior, and align ourselves with what is expected of us. Still, only few of us are able to see ourselves objectively from the outside. Self-assessment is a very difficult thing to do, almost impossible for some. Nevertheless, it is important to step out of your own personality and try to see yourself through the eyes of your colleagues and bosses. There are tools to help you do this. Corporations often use self-assessment and 360-degree assessment (assessment of the individual by superiors, peers, and subordinates) in the talent management and appraisal process. Most of these methods attempt to improve the personality of the individual in preparing them for a more complicated and sophisticated task in the organization.

Corporations want you to give your best for the benefit of the corporation. They motivate, encourage, support, and require taking on challenges. You are more valuable to the corporation if you have sufficient potential to grow: you will retain your experience and use it in a higher context, providing the corporation with added value. The internal talent management process is much more cost-effective and less risky than external hires.

Corporations will push you to take new challenges, perhaps even take a higher position with more responsibility, more complex work. You will consider yourself lucky to be offered the responsibility of whole regions or countries rather than one shop or a large organization instead of a department. Based on your good performance so far, the perception of your personality, and your capabilities, they consider that you'll be able to grow to the new position.

Again, it's all about perception. If you set up an excellent picture of yourself, you will be noticed. You may get a promotion for the second or third time. You might have started as a simple worker but are now being offered the job of operations manager. Or, maybe you joined the company as a mere financial analyst and are now on the way to becoming the CFO. You've done a good job of convincing the corporation to dole out opportunities for you to advance.

NOW, YOU MUST BE ABLE TO SAY WHEN IT IS ENOUGH.

The trick is in your genuine self-assessment, not for the corporation but for yourself. What do you really want? Are you happy, satisfied, and successful in your current position? Will you retain this in a different/higher position, the place where you are aiming to take your career? Will you be able to handle all the challenges you will meet in this new position? How far out of your comfort zone are you willing to go? What is your level of adaptability to handle issues when you are not in your comfort zone? Are you able to become somebody else on a short notice?

You will also have to take into account the corporate world assumption that when you do not grow, you actually decline. This also applies to personal growth. You will be expected to want to grow. You will be given new challenges and expected not only to face them, but also to excel in spite of them.

You must also consider that there are less and less friendly people the higher up you get on that ominous ladder. Truly, it can be lonely at the top, and leaders and senior managers often enjoy golf and business-related social gatherings for this reason. There, they can be among people who are as lonely as they are, and this makes everyone feel better all around.

If you are a friendly gal or chap who likes socializing and thrives on being part of a close-knit team, climbing into a leader position a couple rungs above your comfort zone may not work out for you. You must be aware that you may have to cut close personal ties with your colleagues, as you will become their superior, or perhaps you will be away managing another department. Your subordinates may be hesitant or even afraid to be friends with you. Your once-peers will now be a different breed: you will not be a colleague, but a potential competitor in the race for an even better position. Some may resent your better results or the fact that you are more successful. You will have to watch your behavior and your words – spoken and written – and you will have to learn the high art of business (corporate) politics.

Chapter X - Climbing the Ladder

Many corporate employees go one step further on the corporate ladder than they should, something known to some as "The Peter Principle." (Peter, Laurence J and Raymond Hull.The Peter Principle: Why Things Always Go Wrong. New York: William Morrow and Company, 1969. ISBN 0-688-27544-3). These folks recognize the truth only when they fail in the higher position. There will be ample opportunities to fail and no net of colleagues who will be willing to keep you from falling. A step back is not only humiliating, but also most impractical. What will those around you say when you fail and have to return to your old position, on the rare chance that you'll even be allowed to do so? The corporate world does not forgive failure. The fall is eventually not downward, but out of the corporation. In the end, the unsuccessful employee will need to find another job. If you suddenly lose your job right after a promotion, you will have difficulty explaining this odd set of circumstances in a job interview. Everybody will interpret it as it happened, and your résumé will only highlight the evident failure. Employers want to hire talented, promising, or already successful applicants – not those who just took an embarrassing plunge off the ladder.

You must find the balance between being sufficiently assertive in taking on new challenges and cautiously evaluating your potential promotion. A good compromise is taking on more "horizontal" responsibilities when you feel you've reached your plateau, instead of trying to move higher and higher just for the sake of the climb. This will ensure that you will be considered for further opportunities, still offering growth potential, and at the same time, you will not climb out of your comfort zone and risk a failure that can be fatal to your career.

Chapter Takeaways

• The corporate ladder is one-way climb, and it's a long, hard fall to the bottom.

• Honest self-assessment and knowing your life preferences will help you say no to a risky promotion. Many employees go one step further than they should.

• If you feel you've reached your plateau, do not be afraid to take on more horizontal responsibilities rather than accepting upward promotions.

Chapter XI - Just One Life

Chapter XI – Just One Life

While you are young, ambitious, full of enthusiasm, and single, you are willing to devote to work the better half of a day. You can repeat this routine, singing all the while, even seven days a week. Corporations tend to foster the false perception that commitment is in linear relationship with the length of the workday. Such "committed" members of the company are not only praised, but also celebrated and encouraged. In other corporations, this behavior is even set as a standard. I just hope you are not working for one of those.

I remember when I was painting the ceiling of our new home. I had to answer a half-hour-long phone call with my colleagues in the factory that Saturday because some problem arose and they needed my advice. It took me several years to realize that answering that call was the wrong thing to do. If you are willing to be available for any issue at any time, your colleagues will abuse this and take advantage of your commitment. They will never learn how to solve things alone. Especially, if you lead people, you have to put limits in place. Your subordinates must be able to rely on themselves.

MANAGING THINGS DOES NOT MEAN DOING THINGS.

Management means organizing processes so things are being done without your constant personal interference.

I once led a workshop about systematic work. One of the demonstrating exercises was to connect as many numbers as possible during one minute, according to a certain rule. All participants jumped on the task without thinking and hurried to achieve the highest score. Only one did not move. He just looked at the sheet and thought for almost half the time. Then he started to connect the numbers with incredible speed and achieved the highest score. When I asked him what his method was, he revealed that he had tried to find the system behind the rule. When he realized the system in the spread of the numbers, he could apply the given rules faster, without any major physical effort. In the end, he won the game.

Results are more important than effort. Moreover, you might say that results are really the only important thing in the end. On the other hand, as mentioned earlier, perception and presentation are both very important in the corporate world. The environment must perceive you as hardworking and devoted. We still think excellent results should come from perspiration, extreme effort, and hard work. We believe sitting in front of your computer half the day thinking, then just making some clever moves, a couple of phone calls, and sending some e-mails will not return the same recognition as spending the whole day discussing, negotiating, running here and there, and literally pushing products toward the customer, even if the result is exactly the same. Unfortunately, there are still a lot of organizations where the latter is preferred way of work, even at the managerial level.

I used to work for such a corporation, as a materials manager. Due to the culture of the organization, I put extreme effort and time into micromanaging: several coordination meetings on all topics daily (system precision, stock level, part hot list, logistics issues, delivery delays, etc.), operational management of all problems. The days at work were long; I saw my family only in the evening, and sometimes I was not even able to see my children before they went to bed. As the company worked around the clock, even the weekends were sometimes occupied by trips to work, whenever something popped up that needed my presence at the factory.

One day the lines were down for a part that was supposed to arrive late in the evening. When the truck finally arrived just before midnight, I was waiting at the loading bay. I jumped into it in front of the stock employees to find the parts and hand-carry them to the lines so the machines could start ASAP. Several months later, after our management team gained more experience and momentum, we introduced better planning and management practices. After one year, I rarely had to stay at work later than five p.m. and never waited for parts on late trucks. Instead, I spent more time with fine-tuning the system we built up, in order to handle the daily complications of the operations and ensure on-time deliveries and production support.

You cannot prevent occasional "firefighting" in a crisis period or in a developing company. You should constantly work, however, on building a system that will eliminate the need for firefighting in the long term. Depending on the complexity of the matter, it may take you months or years, but at least you know you will not have to do this forever. Making sacrifices now will glean better results for you later. If the expectation is to spend all your energy and time just to make things work for the present and there is no chance to change, this can be bad. You should question the sanity of such an organization.

A customer once asked why we stayed at work so long. I told him we had many things to do. He asked if we'd have less to do the next day since we'd stayed so late that day, but I told him it would not work out that way, for we had much to do the next day as well. He looked at me curiously and asked, "So what is the point?"

I feel sorry for the workaholics who have no other interest in life beyond their job or work. I accept that there are such people, but I feel great pity for them. Human life is so abundant in possibilities that it seems a waste to expend it only in one dimension. Opponents may purport that if you want to be very good at something, you should spend all your energy and time to sharpen your expertise in that area. Everyone is different though. Some need just one thing, and they can be happy only if they do that and nothing else. They give up family, friends, and the beauties of the world that other people enjoy (traveling, a good book, cultural experiences, parties, hobbies, or anything that makes life richer), and they live for their only interest. You may be one of these, and it is your choice. For workaholics, there is no question of work and life balance, for their life is their work, and vice versa.

I have some remote friends who chose this way of life. They built a spectacular career in the corporate world and made probably a lot of money. They can afford a lot of things that most of us cannot. They experienced fame and recognition but they have not many close friends or a partner with whom they

Chapter XI - Just One Life

can share the experience. They are alone. Are they happy? They say so. They are as happy as a zero-dimensional point moving on a line in one dimension. The spatial point welcomes this one dimension as its whole life. It has no idea about the plane, not to mention the 3D space.

Most of us need more dimensions of life. We are multi-interest personalities that naturally yearn for the privacy of the family life, friends, and the home that makes the antipode of our work life. We want to enjoy nature, go for a walk, play or watch sports, entertain ourselves, and surround ourselves with others to share in our joy of life. Not only do we want to enjoy life every day, but we also build up memories that will serve to later remind us in our old age how rich of a life we've lived. If you are this type of person, you will want to reasonably limit the time and energy you devote to your actual job/work and will crave a balance between it and other activities. If you are able to reach a balance, you will experience that great feeling called happiness.

I will always feel sorry that I did not see my children often enough when they were growing up. I needed to be at work, on business travels, building my corporate career, and there was no other choice. It took several years for me to the balance between family and work, still being successful and recognized, but also enjoying the better side of life.

Some people dread saying no for a corporate requirement that clashes with his or her other priorities, be that family, relaxing, or other enjoyment of life. Your concrete corporate environment will decide what you can afford. You have to evaluate the pros and cons and the danger of saying no. If you never say no, the corporation will consume you, and they will begin to take it for granted. If you say no too many times, your commitment to the corporation will be questioned and finally, you may not be so interesting to them. It is still a better solution to take your laptop with you when you go on holiday and leave your phone switched on, at least during certain agreed-upon intervals. This allows you a limited but efficient connection with issues at work, and you can still enjoy most of your holiday with your family and friends.

I once participated in an important conference call on my cell phone while sitting on some stairs on the island of Capri, Italy, while my family enjoyed Italian ice cream, then coffee, then sweets, then some shopping around those stairs, being more bored with every quarter of an hour. Although I did not see anything of Capri, to be honest, I was with the family and could still do a decent job participating in work matters. Did my family like that? Probably not, but they clearly understood the trade-off and while grumbling, they acknowledged that we still spent a memorable two weeks in Italy that was one of our nicest holidays yet.

A lot depends on the culture of the corporation. The film *The Devil Wears Prada* is an extreme, but not too much exaggerated example of a ruthless corporate culture (here connected to a person) of the overwhelming time, energy, and emotional/mental commitment corporations often require from employees. Your choice depends on you alone, how much of your life you are willing to sacrifice for your corporate career. Fortunately, most corporations will be easier to handle and you can find ways to make a reasonable split between work and life. Ultimately, there are many married successful corporate professionals and managers out there; I know, because I am one of them. You should set limits, however, and refuse to step over them. If the corporation is not willing to accept this, you had better move on before you destroy your life, even if you do not notice it in the beginning. Success in the corporate world does not mean succeeding only in the corporation that will otherwise destroy you.

 ## Chapter Takeaways

- Learn to build a system that works, even in your absence.

- Fight the perception that hard work and devotion means long hours at your desk.

- Unless you are a workaholic, which isn't always healthy, life has more dimensions to it than work. You do not want to feel sorry later that you did not see your children grow.

- Learn to say no when appropriate, but take your laptop with you on holidays and vacations if there is no other way.

Corporate Mission Possible

Chapter XII - Mowing Your Own Lawn

Chapter XII – Mowing Your Own Lawn

Half a century ago, the roadmap of the average university graduate was easy: find a decent job in a medium to large corporation; then use your skills and education to make yourself not only accepted, but also respected and useful; slowly climb the corporate ladder to reach higher and higher positions, gaining financial security along the way; build a nice family and retire well. Job security, although never guaranteed, was definitely better then. The oil and energy crises of the seventies and early eighties, then the financial crisis of the nineties and the dot.com bubble in the late nineties had a turbulent effect on the job market. Some even say the whole of nineties can be called a "world economic crisis," leading to decreasing growth and a changing economic activity, enhanced even more by the fall of the Soviet Union and the socialist economies of Eastern Europe. The latter, however, also meant new opportunities for multinational corporations and expansion to these opening markets.

The global financial crisis of 2007-12 (and we may not be at the end of it yet) depressed economies even more: some claim the current recession is even worse than the "Great Depression" of 1929-32. Job security disappeared, even in large corporations. There seems to be a widespread opinion that instead of relying on jobs in corporations, people should take their fate into their own hands and start up their own ventures, where they can rely on their own capabilities to succeed in the global marketplace. The spread of the Internet, the availability of new technology, and the globalized marketplace made it much easier to build up and succeed in new ventures even for individuals. There are many notable success stories of an average employee leaving her job and, based on a simple idea, built a successful business from scratch in a matter of years. Go to Amazon or any other bookstore, and you will find tens of thousands books claiming to be the ultimate guide to entrepreneurship, guaranteeing that you can make millions right from your living room.

As with everything, there are two sides to the coin – and sometimes even three. It is difficult – and let's face it,

Chapter XII - Mowing Your Own Lawn

impossible – to become a professional football player if you hate running. You can dream of becoming a musician, but if you are tone-deaf, forget it. Entrepreneurship requires being able to sell your product or service, manage your finances, and organize yourself and any employees you later bring in to the endeavor. Unless you have the benefit of a salesperson or advertising department to help you, you will have to look for customers and clientele on your own. You will have to convince them that what they need is your product or service, and you'll eventually have to push them to open their purse. Not all of us have a sales acumen. Some of my friends, although excellent professionals, do not feel comfortable in the selling process, as it is simply not their cup of tea. How can you be successful selling your product or service, albeit you have one, if you actually hate selling?

Corporations, especially large ones, offer a suitable split of jobs and responsibilities. They offer leverage across their large volume. A quality manager, taking care of the correct working of processes when making thousands or millions of products, is well worth the decent salary the corporation pays him or her. On the entrepreneurial stage – as a consultant, for instance – that person will have to build a system, build contacts, and eventually sell services to people. It is a completely different job.

It is not about what is better. It is about what is better for *you* personally. If you feel more comfortable being independent, not affected by anyone's decision, and you don't mind working completely alone, without the help of colleagues, other departments, or the whole organization, you should go for the entrepreneurial stage. If your abilities can be leveraged efficiently only in a large organization, you will have to work around in the jungle of the corporation.

I know quite a number of managers, who, at certain stages of their career, decided to quit the corporate world and start up their own ventures, either as self-employed consultants or running their own small companies in various areas to provide services or products. After several years, although not doing bad, many of them ended up in an other corporate job. They acquired valuable experience and saw the world from the other side, but in most cases, the entrepreneurial setup did not allow them to earn even close to their corporate salary. The pressure of the family, the mortgage, and the lifestyle they were used to eventually broke their initial enthusiasm for their own business.

Pro-entrepreneurship books and advisors often claim that it is much more risky to stay in a corporate job than to set up one's own enterprise. In reality, both are risky, as life always is. The art of survival and success is not about choosing the less risky way; rather, it is about finding ways to mitigate those risks.

In order to succeed in your startup, you will have to plan carefully your choice of markets, products, and services, based on your abilities and potential customers. You will mitigate the risk of bad decisions by evaluating different possibilities, testing products and markets, investing in your venture carefully, and putting into the business extreme efforts to succeed. In the case of your corporate job, you will have to realize the dangers, learn how to behave, communicate, and cooperate to reach maximum effect of your performance. You will have to realize how corporation organizations work and learn the levers of motivation of individuals and departments, the same way as you would need to learn how your market behaves in case of a startup. As a corporate worker, you will have to make compromises on some of your opinions and not always let people know what you think. As an entrepreneur, you will have to serve customers even if you do not like them, and you may not let them know what you think. In the corporation, your boss frustrates you, while competitors frustrate the entrepreneur. You cannot just eliminate either of these.

Chapter XII - Mowing Your Own Lawn

I regret to disappoint you that there is neither hell nor heaven on Earth.

 **Chapter Takeaways**

- Having your own business is not an alternative to working in the corporate world for all. If you are uncomfortable at sales and can leverage your abilities across volume, corporation work is better for you. If you prefer independence and are not afraid of selling, go entrepreneur.

- Corporate jobs are not riskier than owning your own enterprise. Success is about risk mitigation.

- You will always have a boss and will always need to make compromises, even if you have your own business. Customers and competitors cannot be eliminated; if you run your own business, they are, in essence, your bosses.

Corporate Mission Possible

Chapter XIII – Threshold

Everyone has a different threshold for behaviors, actions, and opinions that he or she considers acceptable and in line with personal beliefs. We build our belief system throughout our lifetime, and they change as we grow. Most of us tend to be revolutionary in our teens and early twenties. As we establish families, set and grow our living standards, we tend to become more conformist. Most corporations encourage conformity as opposed to individualism.

In my opinion, generally accepted patterns of behavior do not cover all beliefs that individuals may have. Each of us has some individual beliefs that differ from what the corporation may want us accept. Is it possible to combine our personal beliefs and corporate expectations, even if they are not the same? Can we truly conform?

There are people who will not work in an arms factory because it is against their personal convictions. Whatever you do, even if you explain that those arms are for defense purposes only, you will not change their opinion. In principle, they are against any form of arms, and they certainly will not help build any. This is a trivial case.

I do not doubt that most of us would refuse an invitation to an Aspen skiing weekend or to a Monte Carlo racing trip from a supplier. And what about a drink or lunch? Where is the limit of a friendly encounter, and where do bribes start?

Zero tolerance against bribes and fraud is trivial for honest people. It is not rare, though, that you, as a corporate employee, will be asked to get involved in a less-than-clean operation.

My colleague told me a story of how she, as a financial analyst, found out about certain financial transactions in her company that were not recorded in the official accounting. When she mentioned this to her boss, he declared that she should keep it to herself. As she was not willing to play the whistleblower's role and could not just close her eyes and thus make herself part of the fraud, she decided to quit. It took two

Chapter XIII - Threshold

months, and her boss was fired when the fraud was discovered in an internal audit.

The whistleblower policy (encouraging employees to report dishonest or illegal activities to some specific department or phone number) does not meet some employee's moral standards. Ratting on your colleagues, even if their action is dishonest or fraudulent, is not popular. As in the case above, some employees may choose to get out of the environment rather than informing the internal authorities. The fear that your colleagues might learn that you ratted them out and the threat of insult or isolation may make one think twice. This dilemma is often solved by voluntary escape from the organization.

Mary D. worked for a European corporation as a sales representative, and her corporation was acquired by a multinational. Among the numerous changes that followed, the whistleblower policy of the new corporation was also presented, and all employees were strongly urged to sign the agreement. To rat on her colleagues was so much beyond her moral threshold that she refused to sign the document. She signed her resignation instead.

It is much better if you are in a position to solve the dishonest behavior of the individual yourself. Being the supervisor of the individual gives you means to stop such activities without involving internal authorities. On the other hand, ratting on one's boss has never paid off, as far as I know.

My friend, Greta N., used to work at a respected university (something like a corporation, if you think about it). She was a project manager, and in the financial records, she found evidence of financing the personal activities of the rector from university grants. She had no other choice than to give up her resignation, for she could not force herself to ratting on her boss; at the same time, she was not willing to continue working there, aware of the fraud. The rector later became a candidate of the Senate.

In a certain corporation, the procurement policy requires that all suppliers give payment terms at a minimum of sixty days. Even if the supplier meets this requirement, payments are often paid after seventy or seventy-five days, especially at the end of calendar quarters. The corporation requires employees to hold payments as long as they can, in order to decrease working capital and improving cash flow. The procurement employees have difficulty adhering to corporate requirements, as they feel it is immoral to increase payment terms against agreed duration, especially if it affects a small company that has serious difficulty ensuring the basic sixty days.

The above example is very often practiced in large corporations. Procurement leverage does not mean only price benefits due to volume. Small companies cannot afford to lose high-paying customers, so they tend to comply with long payment terms and reluctantly tolerate such delays, having no other choice. However, what about the procurement employees, if they believe the behavior of the corporation is not ethical?

If you happen to be in a similar situation, you will have to make your own decision. You must acknowledge that as a corporate employee, you are expected to prefer the benefit of the corporation to that of the suppliers. Morals in business are often not the same as in everyday life. It also depends on cultural habits: for instance, Latin nations tend to accept delays in payments, whereas in Germany or Scandinavia, this is unheard of.

If you cannot digest this, you may suggest a policy whereby the corporation will declare that if the suppliers agree to seventy-five-day payment terms, the corporation will guarantee that all payments will be paid within terms, without exception.

Chapter XIII - Threshold

Keeping the word after this potential change then becomes very important; otherwise, the credibility of the corporation will suffer.

Giving your opinion on corporate practices that do not meet your moral standards may sometimes be challenging. Depending on the corporate culture, you may be considered a fool, a troublemaker, or an undesirable. You have to decide if the matter in question hurts your integrity so deeply that you must protest. In most cases, this will not end peacefully. Either you'll make enemies in the process, or the corporation will decide you are not a good fit for them. Eventually this leads to unbearable frustration or a strongly worded suggestion that you should consider resigning. Even if this seems to cost your career, you may not want to work for a corporation with which you do not agree on principle.

If you find yourself in this dilemma, work around it cleverly. Evaluate your position and make your decision without hasty actions. Start looking for another job and when you are ready, take your leave. However, never make the mistake of complaining to your potential new employee about morals at your previous workplace. You will sound too suspicious and your new employee will not believe you. It is better to name other reasons why you left. I made this mistake once early in my career and I failed to secure a good-looking job for myself.

Your corporate career will probe your moral threshold more than once. You should be able to compromise on some of the smaller moral matters that will not significantly hurt your integrity. Otherwise, you will not live long in the corporate world. However, as I stated earlier, everyone has his or her own threshold. I hope you are never forced to step over it, for in the long term, it is not worth it. Making a career is important, but you must also preserve your self-respect, for without that, you will be a bitter person.

Chapter Takeaways

• Your moral threshold may differ from the corporate code of ethics. You must decide whether or not you will be willing to bend your own rules or the code of ethics.

• Giving your opinion on differences between your moral view and corporate practices does not pay off. You must either stomach it or leave.

• You need to compromise on smaller moral matters but safeguard your integrity and self-respect.

Final Words

"So why do you aspire to join us, if you could summarize?"

"Not only will I be able to put my knowledge and experience to good use here, but also enhance my knowledge and take more responsibility as opportunities come my way."

"Why should we hire you?"

"Because I am a very good fit for you requirements, and I would be thrilled to work for my favorite brand name."

"Where would you like to be after three years?"

"I would like to manage the whole department or a large project across the company."

"Have you ever driven a large ship?"

"I have a driver's license for cars and large trucks, and I am sure I can transfer my driving skills to water with a little training."

"Then welcome aboard!"

What are you going to do now in your own career crossroads? Are you frightened by the truths of the corporate world, or are you intrigued by the opportunities this colorful, wide jungle represents for the brave and the savvy?

Here, you have been given somewhat of an inside look at others' experiences in the corporate world. You've witnessed the numerous failures and successes I've seen, including some of my own. I have tried to draw the curtain to let you peek behind the scenes. I have revealed how the motors of the corporate vehicle work and what are the most frequent causes for breakdown.

I understand that not everybody is interested in mechanics. Many have tried hitchhiking without giving a thought to how the driver bought the car, how he maintained it, how he paid for the gas to put in it, or how he drove. Instead, we mindlessly let ourselves be driven toward our destination; when the driver turned another direction, we simply asked him to stop and hopped out to hitchhike in another vehicle.

You are the owner of your career. You decide if you will learn to drive or be driven. When you take over the steering wheel and press the gas and the brake with your own foot, you will take your fate into your own hands. Listening to good advice about how to solve difficult traffic situations will help a lot. Knowing not to jump on the brakes when there is ice on the road is useful, but it is common sense. How to steer, speed up, and safely stop in critical circumstances is another thing entirely. It doesn't only require expert advice, but also details and much trial and error on your own part.

If you have decided to drive instead of being driven, start putting the advice in this book to good use. Start by taking small steps, when situations are not critical but doing things differently might help. Think about your personality and define the corporate image that best fits you. Beware, though, for this is a mask you will have to wear for several hours of your day. it must fit perfectly on the inside, even if it shows a different person on the outside.

Do not forget to take off your mask at home so your smile shines for those you love – the smile of the content and the successful!

One more thing before you go...

If you have questions or opinions to share about the book or its topics, do not hesitate to write to the book's blog:

www.corpjobsuccessguide.com

I will be happy to hear about any suggestions how to make the book better. Please, e-mail me and let me know your suggestions.

If you liked the book, please, leave a review on Amazon.

Thank you!

Rob Mars

rob.mars.author@gmail.com

www.ingramcontent.com/pod-product-compliance
Lightning Source LLC
Chambersburg PA
CBHW060838050426
42453CB00008B/740